BEAUTY'S FIELD

BEAUTY'S FIELD

Seeing the World

Laurence Freeman

CANTERBURY
PRESS
Norwich

Copyright in this volume © Laurence Freeman, 2014

First published in 2014 by the Canterbury Press Norwich
Editorial office
3rd Floor, Invicta House,
108–114 Golden Lane,
London EC1Y 0TG

Canterbury Press is an imprint of Hymns Ancient & Modern Ltd
(a registered charity)
13A Hellesdon Park Road, Norwich,
Norfolk NR6 5DR, UK

www.canterburypress.co.uk

British Library Cataloguing in Publication data

A catalogue record for this book is available
from the British Library

978 1 84825 669 9

Typeset by Regent Typesetting
Printed and bound in Great Britain by
CPI Group (UK) Ltd, Croydon

And dig deep trenches in thy beauty's field,
Shakespeare, Sonnets

Contents

Introduction

'What are you looking for?' These are the first words of Jesus in the Gospel of John. It is also the question that the strong, illuminative moments of life repeatedly present to us. This sense of life as a searching – a relentless looking for something – is repeated until we understand that the question is really a *koan*. The answer doesn't exist except within the change of mind that happens as we seek.

This transformation is sudden and gradual. It emerges when we keep looking for it even if we don't know what it is that we are looking for. It's hard to name what we don't know and 'God' is essentially an unspeakable name. Yet even as the mind opens and perceives that the meaning of life is this *looking for*, the question continues to sound, though more subtly and less agitatedly. If to seek God is to find God, finding God inevitably leads to a new round of seeking. This might sound pointless. But a real and enduring peace of heart comes with this way of seeking.

Maybe this idea of looking for something sounds rather convoluted. But people living in traditional societies, or in communities with respect for received wisdom, know the inherent value of *looking for* and waiting for it to appear, just as they know meaning in the cycle of finding and losing. By contrast, in modern culture, where we are so conditioned by the desire-satisfaction routine of the shopping mall or the Internet, we impatiently demand a factual or material answer to all our questions and feel that every wish must be fulfilled instantly when it becomes conscious.

This book is a collection of moments or short flashes of insight (for what they are worth) that arose in those strong moments when the question of what we are looking for becomes unusually intense: sometimes as a story heard or a personality revealing itself, or a wave of beauty or empathy that comes to us out of the blue. To help the reader hold these apparently unconnected moments together in some kind of pattern it might be helpful to describe the kind of life in which they arose.

It is a life within a monastery without walls. I travel widely but nearly always within the spiritual walls of its cloister, above all visiting our meditation communities and praying with them. Increasingly we use technology to nurture and strengthen this community but there is always a need too for personal visits, especially in emerging countries. Many other teachers share this work with me today but – as a monk with no family commitments and no one at home who really needs me – I have a degree of freedom that allows me to travel widely and frequently.

I can't say I often look forward to each new trip. But once the travelling has started I am aware of how blessed I am to see the work of the Spirit in so many different individuals and cultures and to be enriched and taught by them. I see communities born and struggle and often flourish, and I feel embedded in that process just as I feel welcome whenever I return to my home monastery with walls. As far as I can, I keep the liturgy of the hours as well as my regular times of meditation even on the days of travel. I have learned to use airports as places of prayer. I have little to complain about. As St Benedict says that a monk should be ready to accept the 'meanest and worst of everything', I shouldn't complain anyway even if I was less blessed.

My travels have taught me a lot about the nature of solitude and detachment. But if I describe this life as monastic you might smile as it may not correspond to the popular idea of what monks should be like and how they should live. This conventional image can be a projection of monks as incompetents fleeing a world they cannot, or prefer not to, cope with. This caricature may also merge in and out of another, contradictory idea that sees all monks as mystic beings living in a spiritual world inaccessible to ordinary people. The truth is more nuanced. It also takes account of individuals who, for a variety of reasons, feel called to live out in an explicit way – or try to – the monastic archetype (the one who is looking for) that is in all of us.

When I was a novice I once went to see my mother and said I had to leave by a certain time in the afternoon as we had an important community meeting in the monastery. 'What could you have that's so important to meet about?' she asked. The popular impression of monastic life is that it is either the life of the escapist and deranged or a life in which nothing important happens. As I understood it, however, from my teacher, John Main, it is a life that continuously challenges you to accept wholeness and embrace radical sanity; and it is a life of ongoing transformation. St Benedict saw this, calling the transformation process *conversatio morum*, or a never-ending change of habits and behaviour. For this reason, in the last chapter he calls his *Regula* 'a little rule for beginners'. It's a way to get started and get trained for the 'single-handed combat of the desert'. As Christians look back to the first church of Jerusalem in the generation after Jesus, Benedict looked back to the early, relatively unstructured monasticism of the Egyptian desert as exemplifying the essential principles of the life he was describing. The essential identity of the monk is one who knows that he is 'truly seeking God' and is seen by others to be doing so.

There are, he says at the beginning of the Rule, different kinds of monks. He doesn't approve of wandering monks. This is unlike the Indian tradition that sets the highest value on the *sannyasi* renunciant who abandons all social and religious status and has, like Jesus, 'nowhere to lay his head'. Benedict, writing about coenobitical monks who 'choose to live in a monastery with an abbot over them', prefers to emphasize stability in the cloister although he has many provisions for monks who travel outside.

In fact there are few things Benedict says that monks should do that he doesn't provide an exception for. This has resulted in an exceptionally flexible vision of life alongside a remarkably clear and consistent description of its main values.

A great monastic scholar of the last century, Dom Jean Leclercq, who was an inveterate traveler, used to say, 'I am a very bad monk but I am very much a monk.' I have found that comforting at times but I live nonetheless with a personal tension between *stabilitas* and *conversatio morum*. Over the years of my monastic life I have lived it in a variety of ways from very conventional community living to an increasing degree of solitude. I am not sure how St Benedict would view it but I suppose he would agreed that I have always lived under the obedience to an abbot that he thought was fundamental.

There are many monasteries and other traditional forms of religious life today that look like endangered species. However, new forms of the monastic archetype are also sprouting. In our own 'monastery without walls', formed over the past thirty years by the practice of daily meditation, there is a Benedictine Oblate Community that is attracting contemplatives from different backgrounds and personal responsibilities and that allows them to make different kinds of commitment.

I would like to see a new form of Benedictine life emerge that is based on meditation. Maybe it could also recover some elements of the beautiful Celtic tradition in which monks, oblates and married people form a united community. But I have no doubt that such a new form will have as many differences as similarities when compared with the forms of monastic life with which most people, including monks, are familiar. Somebody asked me recently if I felt I was a success. I thought it was a strange question but realized that I certainly don't and in many ways I feel I have failed. But I am also reassured by the growth and direction of the community that is evolving this new form of Christian contemplative life, in which I belong and to which I am committed until the end of my life.

When I first became a monk I was most fearful of entering a life that would be unrelentingly monotonous and might become merely self-serving. It is a danger of monasticism that it induces a stupor and an evasion of relationship with the world – even between its own members. Monotony, after all, is what it looks like if you just read the timetable on the back of the bedroom door. Each day, with minor variations for weekends and major feasts, looks like a treadmill of sleep, prayer, eating and working. Prayer is inevitably followed by eating and work by sleep. But for me the experience soon proved different. There was more conflict and struggle than I had expected but also a deeply interesting and surprising content to the life. I have known a lot of suffering at times in my monastic life but I thank God I have never been bored. I soon realized – and this reassured me that I hadn't made a wrong decision – that within the little room of the monastic community there are infinite riches, and within its monotone great melodies and harmonies can be heard and deeply felt. However hard it may be, if you don't find monastic life essentially interesting you should reconsider it. Maybe the same is true of marriage; and maybe people stay in monasteries or in marriages long after they have become fundamentally bored with the life but have also become too frightened to leave.

I discovered that contemplative experience is the end of boredom. The incessant stream of entertainment and consumer goods that keep us stimulated in our culture promises novelty but results in a heavy and stagnant *acedia*. Meditation breaks or at least begins to loosen the addictive and compulsive patterns of this superficial way of life that is constantly looking for sensation and yet genuinely *feels* less and less.

The title of this collection of the monthly *Tablet* column that I have written for some years comes from a sonnet by Shakespeare. It evokes the sense I have gained, through my travelling in this monastery without walls, of the world as a field of beauty, constantly renewed even in its mortality. Shakespeare is brutally realistic as he sees that the physical beauty and grace he is contemplating in his beloved will soon show the 'deep trenches', the wrinkles of age. But beauty always points through and beyond the form in which it appears. By means of a small part it gives us an experience of the whole. I could have chosen another poem, by Gerard Manley Hopkins, to evoke what I wanted to suggest here. In 'As Kingfishers Catch Fire' he speaks of his vision in the world of the Christ who 'plays in ten thousand places, lovely in limbs and lovely in eyes not his'. The world is an infinitely interesting, ever-creative place because there is no atom or moment that is not present to us through its source.

I hope these short pieces hang together for you their reader with a certain unity and as a brief celebration of a contemplative way of seeing and rejoicing in the world's blessed diversity.

Laurence Freeman OSB
The World Community for Christian Meditation
www.wccm.org

1

Parallel Universes

It is another world. We are only a few minutes' drive from the city but already on the edge of civilization. Mauricio is driving the van that he uses to deliver food and clothes to the people he helps; he is a retired architect, inspired by the Little Brothers of Jesus; he now spends half his time at the *favella*. He is impassioned, dramatic. We bump along uncomfortably up the road as the green hills of Minas display postcard beauty. No tourists come here. At the top of the hill we park by a large white cross erected on the spot where, in 1986, the tortured bodies of three boys, two 14 and one 16 years old, had been found laid out mockingly in a circle. The police had tried to extract the names of their bosses in the *traffico*, the drug trade. They had taken them to this beautiful, quiet place where their screams would not be heard.

Mauricio tells me that the police had learned these methods during the years of Brazil's military dictatorship. The threat – for the landowners – of land reform passed and the country returned to democracy. But the virus of police corruption and violence continued to drive an ever-wider wedge between law and justice. I realize, with my memories of London policemen on the beat, how difficult it is to imagine such a fundamental gap in social trust. As the poor from the northeast began to migrate south looking for work, the *favellas* formed, mirror images, parallel universes beside the cities they descended on and infiltrated. But until the 1980s the *favellas* were seen as romantic places. The young of the middle class went there for real samba, for *carnevale*, for evenings out.

Now they come just to buy their drugs. Even today, long after they came of age in the drug era, the *favellas* themselves look magical at night. At a safe distance, their lights sparkle enticingly up and down the hillsides. But these worlds turn sinister when darkness falls. Last year I was visiting a meditation group in a *favella* in Rio. As the afternoon shadows lengthened the priest asked us if we would be disturbed when, soon after mass, the evening shooting would start. He saw my companions' look of fear and suggested that we leave then and advised us to keep the lights on inside the car as we drove out.

Brazilians are not a violent people. Their history has few wars. They like to make their living doing what they most like to do. They love music, ideas and conversation, religion in various syncretistic forms, the beach and, of course, *futebol*. A film like *City of God* captures something of the tragic self-contradictions of this world of multiple universes. A people impassioned with life and celebration, sensual and spiritual, their music and sport transcends racial and social divisions. Yet they have got used to hearing of the shootings of children, and of police helicopters swooping down in the *favellas*, spraying bullets into crowded streets. The poor, who were once an object of pity and charity, are now feared. The two worlds fly ever further and more dangerously apart.

We join hands around the cross and pray for the boys killed there and for all who suffer alone and unheard. It seems some consolation, some sign of giving meaning to those young, wasted, pain-flooded lives. But as we drive away I speak with a priest who has spent the past 28 years living in the *favella*. Unlike Mauricio, he is quiet and deep and tired. He has no solutions, no dreams. The comforting sense of consolation we all indulge seems to have dissolved. His hope is visible just in presence, his being present to the victims of this crazy, unjust universe of drugs, poverty and violence. When he hears of someone arrested he goes down and sits in the police station. Every hour or so he gets up and asks the policeman at the desk for an update. It lets them know that their prisoner has a name and a friend. Does it help that he is a priest? He smiles and says it is better the police don't know that he is.

Mauricio leads us down a steep dirt track past cinder-block houses to one that he built over three Saturdays. For someone, each of these poor dwellings surrounded by garbage is a dream come true. Patricia greets us at the door of her house, a beautiful but worn 30-year-old who had been abandoned as a child by her mother and grew up on the streets. She gave birth to the first of her own three children on the street. Miraculously she met a man who accepted her with her children and stayed with her. Even more miraculously Mauricio found them and helped lift them into a better world. She tells her story with dignity. Making soap brings a few *reals*. Her husband leaves each morning, like the labourers in the parable, to find or not find work. She does not like being dependent on Mauricio for help, but she often has to sell the money for the soap-making materials to feed the children. It is much better than the streets. She has a tap and a fridge and a magnet of Mickey Mouse on the fridge door. There was hope but not much more. I wonder if her children will avoid the temptation when they see the drug dealers, who trade openly on the streets, flash their money at them and offer an easy and quick way into a better world.

We take a picture with Patricia, which she enjoys, and then drive back to the city. We meet with the Archbishop, have a pizza, say vespers, give an evening talk at the university. The next morning in the paper I see a photo of a 14-year-old Palestinian boy, a foiled suicide bomber. He is kneeling, stripped, terrified under the guns of Israeli soldiers. His posture is just like that of Christ in Massacio's painting of the Baptism. Something that it is very hard to define unites the different universes we inhabit.

March 2004

2

Fat Ladies of Malta

I was captivated by the fat ladies of Malta. Sitting or lying, their rolls of fat shamelessly piled on each other, hips, breasts, legs all flowing into each other like mountain ranges. Shocking, in a world where obesity seems about to be criminalized. The Maltese fat ladies, however, are not just obese. No one knows how old they are, but being at least 4,000 years old they are beyond fashion and law. Their stone figurines are the oldest known human image of God: God as Woman, Mother, all-embracing Nature. For much longer than God the Father has so far reigned, the Divine Mother once dominated the human imagination and impregnated every aspect of life with her religion. In her there happened a re-linking of earth and sky, human and animal, death and life and of the cycles of all kinds of growth.

Malta also boasts the oldest lintel in the world – an invention as simple as the wheel and as revolutionary. But for our Neolithic ancestors doors were also religious symbols. As you walk through what remains of the prehistoric temples on Malta, weaving between their massive rough-hewn stones, you try to imagine what it once looked like. Suddenly, looking at the archaeologist's plan, you see it from within. It flashes on you that you have already passed back into the Mother. The doorway is the entrance welcoming you into her chthonic womb. Just as churches are a cross, these temples are fat ladies. Seeing this, you might shiver, a brief, stabbing connection with ancient energies that you can feel but that your modern, disenchanted mind lacks something to understand. It is the same unnamable, numinous thing that you will find at Stonehenge where, on the summer solstice, modern druids dress up in Arthurian robes and worship the ever-dying sun; or at the burial mound at New Grange in Ireland, built before Abraham left Ur of the Chaldees, where the first rays of the newborn sun at the winter solstice penetrate the darkened inner chamber; or in the painted prehistoric caves of Lescaux where the great graffiti illustrates their sense of identity with the animals they had to kill in order to live; in all these places we *feel* the mystery but *understand* very little. What those ancestors of ours (less than a hundred generations ago) actually believed and how they worshipped and what the more thoughtful among them personally felt about it all, we will never know. They left us their shrines and graves but no words.

Perhaps this belief is what most impresses us in a post-religious western world where our temples are shopping malls and reality television shows our liturgies. That they believed anything so totally and that their belief united every aspect of life from child rearing to farming, from the making of domestic utensils to burying the dead, this is hard to relate to. Is *belief* even the right word to describe so integrated, embedded, a spirituality? If we are right, that they did see and experience life through such a simple, perhaps unquestioned and yet unifying lens, is it not all the more eerie how completely it has all been lost and forgotten? The buildings and figurines are still here but we are not there any more where they had meaning.

Suddenly you're beamed back to today. Leaving the temple there is a big noticeboard with the European Union logo. Malta joined that golden circle and became a member of the new Europe in 2004. The board proclaims new regulations governing the maintenance and entrance rights to the shrines of the Divine Mother and all other archaeological sites in its jurisdiction.

Some of the nicest fat ladies are in the Valletta museum of Maltese history. Valletta is one of the huge sun-whitened fortress towns that make up the urban life of this island of about 300,000 souls and the many transient, less soulful tourists that fuel its economy. It is an excellent museum guiding you from the time when Malta was physically connected to Sicily and continental Europe, through the era of the fat ladies, past Phoenician traders and Arab invaders, Crusader Hospitaller Knights, Napoleon's failure to subdue the people by destroying their religion, England's gentler rule, resistance to German bombers, and so into the Age of Tourism. At the end of the timeline diagram, the culmination of all that has been, the end of history, there is entry into the European Union (thanks to a majority of 1 per cent in the referendum).

All proclaimed finalities are illusory. The idea about the 'end of history' became briefly fashionable after American victory in the Cold War and the acclaimed global dominance of democracy and free markets. Today, as the 'war against terror' self-destructively threatens the western democracies themselves, it seems a very foolish thought. But it is a recurrent illusion to believe that we have arrived at the end of the line. Here in Malta, though, where history is so layered and laid out to view, time seems to revolve in a big, slow cycle, not only as a shooting arrow. The massive fortresses of the Knights, the 'monks of war', the sun-drinking plains between, the low flat-roofed houses that remind you just how close they are to the Arab world, everything reminds you of the waves of war that have swept successively over this island. It is the karma of violence that hovers heavily in the air of the soul and of the culture. It is a relief to remember the fat ladies when, so the pre-historians assure us, there was no war because God was a fertile, nurturing Mother, terrible but not military, not a warrior demanding the extinction of the enemy's children.

And the Church? Christ came when St Paul was shipwrecked and spent six months here on his way to Rome. Much later, the Knights of Malta came, devoutly committed to the eradication of the infidel, as certain of God's approval as al-Qaeda today. Malta became a theocratic state again. As late as the 1970s the Arch-

6

bishop excommunicated the Prime Minister and denied church burial to members of the Labour party.

Even today there is no shortage of priests. On the small sister island of Gozo one parish alone has 20. Saying mass is a competition, so one wealthy family built its son a church of his own, although the bishop has so far declined to consecrate it. The Maltese are devout, yet thoughtful and strong willed. Thirty per cent go to daily mass, at least 80 per cent on Sundays. Surely Malta is the last truly religious country in Europe? But now many Maltese are asking what will be the effect of this latest end of history on their future. Will the rich, quirky, sturdy identity of this small island people, psychologically as deep and broad as a continent, that has survived so many invaders, be able to resist the super-virus of secular consumerism that has, everywhere else, swept everything before it?

Dietrich Bonhoeffer looked into the visions of the night as he faced his death in 1945 and his own faith in Christ bloomed. He wondered prophetically about a coming 'religionless Christianity'. He meant, I think, an integrated Christian spirituality lived in a society that was no longer, and never could again be, religious as religion was once understood. In Europe, Australia and North America today this is the new reality that the Church faces. Asian Christians will face it soon. Religious people may assume an aggressive, fortress mentality, as the Knights of Malta once did, but history always wins in the end. You flow with it or you are swept away by it. Even if you think you are saving the world by resisting it, you may find you were merely trying anxiously to save yourself. Nothing is emptier than a temple that has lost its meaning

Amid the gloomier of these reflections I found hope in a typically untypical Maltese lay community whose priest-founder has been beatified. It pervades the whole society with men and women of pure dedication and great talent serving the spiritual growth of the young. About 80 per cent of Maltese children pass through their programmes. It enjoys a high reputation everywhere. It is rooted in the tradition of faith and yet open to change. Before I left I met and meditated with some of the young people they were teaching. They were bright, questioning new Europeans who valued their rare gift of an intact, inherited faith. But they were becoming self-conscious about it too. With the searching gaze of the young, sifting the real from the phony, they seemed to be standing on the shoulders of the fat ladies and of all their varied pasts.

Temples, languages, beliefs and whole cultures can pass from memory. The young, as they should be, were looking ahead rather than back, and the fat ladies, who can look both ways even while lying down, were smiling on them.

June 2004

3

Monte Oliveto Maggiore

In the dry heavy heat of a Tuscan afternoon the bus drops off retreatants from several continents. They now have to walk carefully down a steep path towards the guesthouse and monastery. The path is a parable: made of slim, ancient terracotta bricks, many crumbling, some missing or replaced with new ones. The stone underfoot, like the pale red brick of the fourteenth-century monastery, is so worn and warm it looks and feels soft. Even as they watch their step down the beaten path they see the views over the wooded valleys and breathe in the pungent scent of *ginestra*. They are also worried about their bags and wondering what their rooms and food will be like. But they are already forgetting London, Houston, Singapore and Geneva and, to their surprise, they have already begun to feel at home. They have arrived.

I have seen this for 20 years now, the reactions of those coming for the first time to the annual silent Christian meditation retreat at Monte Oliveto Maggiore, the mother house of the Olivetan Benedictine Congregation, south of Siena. Like being introduced to a startlingly beautiful person, the outrageous physical beauty of the place is unexpected, even at first disturbing. The peacefulness, the self-confidence of the place and the at-homeness of the white habited monks who live here becomes if anything more amazing as you get used to it. There are not many places in the modern world where there is such a combined sense of stability, harmony and hospitality. Your first thought might be that it is so much of a home to someone else that *you* are condemned to being an outsider. But it proves to be one of those rare places that has the grace of making everyone feel at home – meaning you feel you can let go, be yourself and take time to remember who you are.

The monks, their rhythm of prayer and eating, processing from choir to refectory, and in between preparing intensely for both activities, are easy with the place and its beauty, hospitable to their guests and tolerant of the tourists. Their danger is complacency but their strength is kindness. They are no longer saying 'how beautiful!' all the time, of course, but they are pleased, even reassured in their own personal struggles to see the visitors fall in love with it. The retreatants have their own schedule of meditation, conferences, mass and yoga, and free time in the afternoon to walk the hills.

The faith of a young investment banker expands in an environment without competition and a timetable without hurry. For the tired social worker there is time and space to become conscious of the source of compassion. The cancer patient can question and do *lectio*, but also not think and be silent. It seems a great luxury and yet is not. Everything is simple, moderate, gently disciplined. At dinner we talk, enjoying the diversity of a community that finds unity and friendship in silence. We end the day by joining the monks for compline. This year the Sunday coincides with the feast of St Benedict so we all go to a liturgy with a long Italian homily and rhetorical speeches to the visiting prelates. But even the formal worship is done casually, with the ease of people who are at home.

With so much religious fundamentalism in the air, it is enlightening to find a deeply religious environment which welcomes people of diverse views and cultures. It doesn't immediately pounce on differences or apply labels of approval or exclusion. It doesn't judge harshly or condemn or acquit in the name of Christ or Allah or Yahweh. I feel it is this, the friendship of the body with the mind in an environment of natural beauty, the surprise of friendship found in contemplation with strangers, the being together in a living stream of tradition that has not been dammed and stagnated, that makes people feel at home.

God, as Aelred of Rievaulx bravely said, is not only love. God is friendship, with oneself, others and the environment. Those who are not in friendship can know nothing of God. In the cruel certainties of the religious bigot defending God against his enemies this friendship has been forgotten. The anxious homelessness of our fragmented society has engendered a contemplative homing instinct even deeper than fundamentalism. In a place like this, the homing instinct for God intensifies in the presence of human warmth, tolerance, hospitality and a more gentle kind of religion. It is in the spiritual search of our time to long for such a feeling of connection and mutual trust, for a religion that nurtures community rather than division. Perhaps it is this inclusive, catholic sense of being at home with difference that reveals the meaning of the real presence.

When Bernardo Tolomei, a rich nobleman from Siena, came here to seek God 700 years ago he was abandoning a comfortable home for what was then seen as a dangerous wilderness. He lived in prayerful solitude and, when companions joined him, adopted the Rule of St Benedict. St Catherine of Siena, a Joan Chittister of her day, berated him, just as she lambasted bishops and clergy for their lukewarmness, for accepting too many monks from wealthy families, and he obediently widened his vocation base.

Like other men she criticized, Bernardo was not above being taught by a woman. Men and women, even in the monastic life of the time, seemed more at home with each other. When plague struck Siena he left his new contemplative home and returned to care for the dying in his old city where he too was infected and died. In the zen ox-herding story, the seeker returns to the marketplace after his enlightenment. The cycle of St Bernardo's monastic journey shows that the peaceful sense of being at home is not self-centred. Nor is it restricted to one place. The more at home you feel, the more you can let go of it. If you really are at home with yourself in God you will find yourself at home with others. Regard-less of geography, you will feel a wave of compassion uniting you to those in need.

The sense of homecoming that I and others feel in returning here to Monte Oliveto teaches me this, each year more beautifully.

August 2004

4

The Wedding

It was a golden summer evening on the banks of the St Lawrence River and a celebration not only of their love but of the blessings of family and the riches of friendship. The wedding was, coincidentally, on the thirteenth anniversary of their first meeting (when they were both 16). As in all good liturgy, the sacramental moment, the exchange of vows, came as prepared for yet still seemed improvised. Sam had been worried for Jen who didn't like speaking in public. But, when they looked into each other's eyes and spoke their carefully crafted marriage vows to each other, it was he who choked up. Maybe he had seen his father in the front row, crying. When I realized that I had forgotten the few minutes of silence that Sam and Jen had asked to follow what they referred to as my 'philosophical discourse' (pc for 'sermon'), I whispered to him asking if he wanted it now. 'No, let's get outa here,' he whispered back.

Twenty years ago Sam had been in a children's meditation group that met on Saturday mornings at the monastery. Now he is a famous rock star with a social conscience. He had just returned from a visit to Mexico organized by a TV station to investigate the sweatshops. He was soon to set off on an international tour for his new CD. When he called to ask if I would marry him and Jen, I asked if it had been a hard decision to take, after their long relationship. 'No, not hard,' he answered, 'it just took a long time. I know we are made for each other.' I said I would be happy to come but asked him to handle the ecclesiastical paperwork with his local church. There was a silence. 'Well, we weren't thinking of a church wedding … In that sense … necessarily.' Evidently he, too, after ten years of Catholic schooling, did not naturally look to *the Church* to express his spiritual life. For them the marriage seemed a mystical not a legal event. They are actually quite traditionally oriented young people. But the regulations hedging the Church's sacramental life seemed to them about as personal and spiritual as airport security screening. It had robbed the sacraments of their power to bless the natural and domestic mysteries of life.

In the end, however, as we composed the ceremony and they wrote their vows, we reinvented the wheel. This is not a bad thing if it reminds us what wheels are for. I remember as a child having my Catholic mind burst open on hearing the obvious – that God made the mass for human beings not human beings for the mass. Conditioned to see sacraments as an obligatory sacrifice of time that God demanded for his own rightful honouring, this was a completely new and liberating perspective. At Sam and Jen's wedding, as we flowed in the long golden evening from the ceremony to the reception to the dinner, I again saw how liturgy is of the people for the people by the people.

Once, when I was participating in an Anglican funeral of an old friend, both of mine and of the elderly vicar officiating, we stood beside each other in the graveyard as the coffin and mourners filed past and I noticed the old priest was weeping. I offered a word of comfort. 'You will miss Gordon.' 'Yes I do,' he sobbed, 'but that's not it. I just realized: I am retiring next month and this is probably … the last funeral I will perform.'

Before the Sam Roberts band started up I was cornered by a middle-aged guest with a 'why I never go to church any more' story. Fortunately I don't have space here to tell it all but it culminated in the account of the priest presiding at his grandmother's funeral who refused to allow the mourning family to offer even a short eulogy. His explanation was, 'We are here to say a proper funeral mass, not canonize anybody.' Priests have their purpose. But whose funerals, whose weddings are they?

The anecdotal evidence and the statistics of disaffection with formal religious ceremony are illustrated by diving church attendance. People feel less and less that the sacraments are made *for them*, to help them express the ineffable presence of God in their lives at the big milestone moments as well as in the daily and weekly routines. Church for many now seems an insiders' club whose rules they cannot understand. It exists increasingly for the sake of the people who regulate it. The security industry similarly seems to have separated from the people it is meant to protect, from the director of Homeland Security down to the sad looking agent who searches your bag at the X-ray machine. Is all this security, all this liturgical policing, really necessary? Regulation is necessary but easily grows under its own logic to kill the very thing it is supposed to be protecting and serving. The goal of the liturgy according to the Council is to 'develop a contemplative orientation' in the people of God. Worship in spirit and truth.

Sam and Jen's wedding expressed an archetype – marriage – in a typically modern way. It touched into and, as quantum physics says, also briefly effected a 'precipitation' of the usually unnoticed mystery of reality into the material world. But it needed symbolism to do this meaningfully and the tradition nearest to the couple was able to channel some. Why else do people treasure the photos and videos of wedding days and baptisms throughout their lives?

Weddings cheer everyone up because, unlike funerals which conclude tragedies, nuptials insist that life is, in the highest sense, a self-perpetuating comedy. This is why Sam and Jen were their own celebrants, and Sam after all is a professional performer. They helped the rest of us there to see that all of life, lived consciously, is sacramental, breathing mystery through symbols, if we have eyes to see and ears to hear. The sacred in us strains for expression. The mystery itself cannot be regulated. 'There is no law dealing with such things as these,' as St Paul remarked about the fruits of the Spirit.

September 2004

5

Boxing Day

'Father, give me a word,' the desert monks would ask their elders. 'Go to your cell and your cell will teach you everything,' was the formulaic response, but given after the elder had listened to the novice's confession and his problems.

'Two loves I have …' said Shakespeare. And I have two monasteries, one with and one without walls. Today I am safely behind the one with. Before Christmas I changed my cell to the adjoining one because it has better bookshelves, and a decent interval has now elapsed since the death of its last occupant, the saintly and much revered Abbot Vittorino. The room is filled with his equanimity. Having laboriously moved everything and settled in, I then, like all monks down the ages, sat in it and wondered what to do next.

Today is Boxing Day. A cold bright sun is drenching the garden and spilling into the monks' rooms. Listening to Dire Straits' 'Brothers in Arms', I look out of the window at the bare trees and am startled to see the symbol of the World Community for Christian Meditation (my other wall-less cloister) sitting high on a branch. Not, it is true, the two white doves of our logo, but two exceedingly plump London pigeons. They are, however, in the classic pose, one looking outward and the other inward. Martha and Mary. Active and contemplative. It is an archetype found first expressed, as far as I know, in the Upanishads: 'There are two birds, two sweet friends, who dwell on the self-same tree. The one eats the fruits thereof, and the other looks on in silence.' I recognized it too in the fourth-century chapel of San Vitale in Ravenna in a mosaic of two doves sitting on the edge of a chalice. Here it is again making a fleeting suburban appearance in North London.

My attention is distracted from this epiphany of the archetype as, a few rooms away, the balcony door opens and Dom Benedict, ever ancient ever new, emerges into the cold fresh air. He makes a hasty sign of the cross and proceeds to do what he might not like me to call a yogic salutation to the sun, his brief and rather stiff but regular morning exercise, arms up and down, some deep breaths and back indoors.

At the parish mass at 8.30 this morning, the Feast of the Holy Family, I quoted Tolstoy's opening to *Anna Karenina*. 'Happy families are all alike. Every unhappy family is unhappy in its own way.' But I hope every family can, in its unique and universal way, taste the same happiness that a monk feels – from time to time – in his world.

Today we could as well be celebrating the Holiness of the Family. In the vision of the gospel there are no hierarchies of vocation. One of the ancient strengths of Catholicism is that it always recognized and defended Mary's monastic and contemplative calling in contrast to that of Martha, her active sister, who in the story shows what happens to us when activity becomes stress and self-alienation. It is one of our weaknesses historically to have pretended that professional virgins are inherently closer to God. One of the World Community's patrons, the late Cardinal Jean Margeot, was appointed head of the Commission on the Family by Paul VI. He told me that when the Pope gave him the job he said that the spirituality of the family was vital to the Church's future because the vision of the Council could only be realized by a contemplative laity. The two plump pigeons, the two white doves, the two sisters, single and married, clergy and laity.

If this vision of a contemplative–active Christianity in the world is realized and if the prophetic spirit of the Council is to be fully implemented, then somehow the relationship of monks and nuns, single and married, clergy and laity needs to express the equality and complementarity of all their vocations. They need to learn how to help each other fulfil their particular call to that same experience of happiness that we call, a little dangerously, holiness.

Yesterday, Christmas Day at Cockfosters, we continued one of our traditions that express this vision. For over 60 years it formed a local monastic church at the end of the Piccadilly line. The founder, a prophetic Belgian monk, Abbot Constantine Bosschaerts, contributed to the Council through a passion for Christian unity which he shared for a period with the future John XXIII as a friend and secretary. The monks and parishioners of Christ the King, Cockfosters, host Christmas dinner for people alone at home, bereaved or burdened with a demanding role as principal carer for a spouse or parent. It is the best illustration of Matthew 22 that I have seen: 'Go out to the thoroughfares and invite everyone you can find to the wedding. The servants went and collected everyone they found, good and bad alike.' To me yesterday they all seemed good. But best of all was the old couple I sat with. He was very infirm, his wife strong and humorous in a valiant London way. When he coughed on his food and sprayed it out together with his false teeth, which landed in my plate, we helped her mop him up with much laughter, and then ourselves. In the way she coped there was the compassion, care and humour of holiness, grace; whatever you call it, it was the real thing.

The desert fathers were right, your cell teaches you everything, especially when you see that your cell is the branch on which the two birds sit together and, at special moments, become one.

December 2004

6

Love and Death in a Canadian River

While Presidents tremble, terrorists threaten and megastars seek more limelight; while some grieve the loss of old friends and suffer the rearrangement of their soul; while others pursue their careers or plan their retirement; the salmon are running on the Goldstream River in British Columbia, the Saanlich inlet from the ocean, as they have done for longer than even the native peoples remember. These lusty fish (male and female he created them too) swim upstream against the fast-flowing current over rocks and fallen branches. It is the beginning and the end of their life cycle because they come here to spawn, to fertilize and then to die.

It is a semi-tropical, humid walk along the river banks through this stretch of the temperate rainforest of Vancouver Island. An easy outing, many schoolchildren and visitors come at this time of year to watch the salmon's cold passion for survival and their ready sacrifice of their individual selves. If fish have selves. A friendly woman ranger approaches us, eager to tell us what she knows and to answer our questions. She hears our English accents and soon we learn she came here from Surrey at the age of 12. Her home it appears was just round the corner from where one of us now lives. 'Amazing', of course, and 'amazing' is the response to all that she has to tell about this great theatre of nature that is being performed for us.

The fish have to wait in the estuary until sufficient water fills the river before they can begin their passion. As soon as they do, precise physical processes begin to unfold. One type of salmon undergoes a jaw mutation as it battles upstream so that, for some reason I didn't understand, it can't eat. Maybe hunger makes it more desperate to survive and procreate. Nature adapts for protection or pollination. But the same fate awaits them all.

The males heroically fight each other to the end. Many have visibly damaged fins and tails; like old battered boxers, they never stop competing. Others grow sharper teeth for this last battle for the right to fertilize the eggs. These are spawned by the females and deposited in 'redds', the holes scoured out by rapid tail motion over the silt on the river bed. The successful male who has cornered and territorialized his chaste bride then has about a minute to drop his contribution into the redd. Neither has eaten anything since their run began. Soon after the spawning they both begin to die, first changing colour into a ghostly white. The sides of the river are littered with their corpses, which provide easy meals for the eagles and a fascinated, delighted horror to the city kids.

And then to add to the drama there are the cross-dressers. These are the more puny male salmon that would get beaten up by their macho peers and so disguise themselves as females by growing an identifiable black line on their side. It gives them a better chance of fulfilling their special duty before they too must expire. Everyone dies. But the fertilized eggs grow in their cosy redds until the fry appear in the spring and head downstream to the sea. In their beginning is their end. And, to quote Eliot again, as his Sweeney Agonistes says, it is all disturbingly and mystifyingly simple: 'birth, copulation and death'.

In the log-built visitor centre there are souvenirs and postcards of wildlife, furry fox cubs and soaring eagles. Around a roaring open fire a group of children are being addressed by a young warden. They are enthralled as she communicates her enthusiasm and wonder. Behind them is a screen linked to an underwater camera and whenever a fish appears the children erupt. Feeling hungry with all this fresh air and thinking of smoked salmon we start to move on, but then we hear the young ranger ask the children, 'And what's it all for? Why are the salmon here?' As I would very much like to know, I go back and join the class. I learn from some of the more precocious children that it is because the salmon form part of a bigger picture, the whole ecological system of the earth.

Then it clicks. I realize what is most amazing about all this is not really the details of the life cycle of salmon even with its eerie evolutionary anticipations of *Homo sapiens* that make us wonder what we really are. What is amazing is that we are all here, so interested, investigating, visiting, buying souvenirs, watching webcams of dying fish. Is this 'ecological system' the 'great chain of being' we lost belief in? Now we don't speak of the first link in the chain, but under different guises myth – even in a demythologized world – does what myths are supposed to do: entertain, astound and explain the Story we are all part of and belong to.

The first teachers believed that God wrote two books to explain everything, creation and the Bible. Contemplation begins with nature and ascends to God. But even in the contemplation of the natural world self-consciousness is transcended in wonder. But nature reasserts itself. Having learned why the salmon are here the children realize they are hungry too and, like us, leave for lunch. Unobserved and unapplauded the fish continue to swim, on and off the screen.

November 2004

7

HHDL

Sitting with the Dalai Lama in an overheated room in Belfast last week, for a series of meetings with political leaders, watching him adapt to the different personalities and trying to understand their views (and accents) and seeing their attraction and warm trust towards him, I was reminded of these words of Isaiah: 'How beautiful upon the mountains are the feet of him that brings the message of peace.' Some years ago I heard Cardinal Piovanelli, then Archbishop of Florence, apply these words in his thanks to the Tibetan Buddhist leader and Nobel Peace Laureate after an interfaith service. I felt proud of my church at that moment. I heard one of its leaders draw from his inner well of scripture words that showed he could recognize the eternal Word alive and active outside his own visible boundaries. Christianity at that instant showed itself truly catholic, confident, inclusive and truly religious, free from the egotism and the narcissism of small differences that bedevils institutions and sects.

The Dalai Lama was in Northern Ireland for three days of the Way of Peace. This is a regular programme of The World Community for Christian Meditation that brings contemplative awareness and inter-religious friendship to bear upon the global work of peace-building. He first visited Northern Ireland in 2000 with the World Community and was enthusiastically greeted by most sections of the society, from Peter Mandelson, then Secretary of State, to the street kids of West Belfast. This time the official welcome was less overt because of the intimidation that China was able to exert on Britain and other western governments hungry for trade deals. But leaders of each political party responded warmly to an invitation to meet him privately, to share their views on the peace process and to listen to his wide and wise global perspective.

He has a rare gift – maybe it is associated with the fact that he has nothing to threaten people with – for evoking a trusting human response even in the most formal of situations. One leader who had recently suffered a personal loss asked for a few moments alone with him. Another politician associated with an intensely sectarian party opened a bag containing the Dalai Lama's books and asked him to sign them. One after another they thanked him for coming and broadening their perspective. No one knows better than leaders of Northern Ireland, where children have recently invented the pastime of 'recreational rioting', the consequences of narrow-mindedness. Perhaps encountering a mind as broad and clear as this Tibetan monk's offers them both solace and hope.

The Dalai Lama told them he had nothing to gain by coming to Northern Ireland. But simply as a human being it pained him to see conflict and violence linked to religion. It baffled him that the (to him) relatively minor differences between Catholics and Protestants could produce such hatred and he pointed, by contrast, to his dialogue with Christians. If he, a non-theist, could be friends with believers didn't that say something about how differences could be seen as bridges not divisions?

I wondered why these politicians, together with the Corrymeela Community that he visited and the civic leaders he spoke with in the Waterfront Hall, all liked him so much and trusted him so deeply. As he spoke with Gerry Adams and Sinn Fein I saw them disarmed – in another sense of the word – by his truthfulness and simplicity. He is not what they expected a global celebrity to be like. What they received by meeting him was more than the photo op they might have calculated for.

All true authority is bestowed by those whose interest that authority is meant to serve. When an element of force, threat or fear enters the relationship, authority is corrupted. It is not inherited by blood or decree. It cannot be imposed. Guile or coercion dissolves it. The Dalai Lama's commitment to non-violence runs deep into his personality. He has, at great cost, put this principle into policy and his policy into practice. Despite the glitz of celebrity that most politicians and even religious leaders might secretly envy, he is genuinely humble, down to earth and touchable.

He *communicated*, with rare personal directness, with the thousand people in the Church of Ireland cathedral at the concluding meditation service and did not forget the hundreds standing outside for whom there was no room; but he does not *work* a crowd. He seems really to love the people he sees and would genuinely like to know and greet each one. His joy – in Buddhist thought joy is produced by insight into *emptiness* – is contagious. The anxiety of many leaders to defend or augment power is lacking in the Dalai Lama. Perhaps this is why he is listened to with more trust and affection than any politician and most clergymen. Perhaps it is the powerlessness from which he speaks that is his authority. His secret is that he has no secret. He has the trappings of celebrity but he is a refugee without a passport or diplomatic credentials. He has nothing and can bequeath nothing except what he gives today. His existential poverty is seen in meeting with the President of the United States a few days before with the same equality as he tossed a basketball with children from both churches in Belfast.

When I am with him I think of the description of the Wanderer from the *I Ching*, the Chinese book of wisdom: 'A wanderer is one who seeks. Strange lands and separation are his lot: success through smallness.' His smallness is immense. His success is not political or economic. After 50 years of occupation and genocide his country faces cultural extinction. Politicians meet him if it suits them but none dare now to raise the Tibet issue with the Chinese.

Maybe this powerless greatness is why, as a Christian, I see the Christ manifested in him and why, as a monk, I see him as one of the few teachers I have known who simply to be with and observe is to be taught.

November 2005

8

Eva Peron and San Miniato

What do Eva Peron, the Argentinian political diva who died in 1952, and San Miniato, the third-century martyr, have in common? Immediately, just that in the same week I visited both their graves. Eva's in a large Buenos Aires cemetery, and San Miniato's in the dark crypt of the church of his name that overlooks the city of Florence. Every life is a story, even if there is never a musical made from it or a church built to celebrate it. In these two stories personal reality has been consumed by legend. Story became myth. What Greek warriors happily died for, at the price of dying young, they achieved: fame beyond the grave.

I met Eva in the musical *Evita*, which universalized what had been an intense but local cult of populist sainthood. To those who loved her she was holy. To those who didn't she was a fraud dragged up from the gutter by her looks and charms. The music's blend of tango, pop and jazz illustrates the palette of her seductive appeal. She was born illegitimate, into poverty, and claimed that every memory of her early life was dominated by a sense of injustice. As a beautiful actress she captivated Juan Peron, then a rising star in the army. They married and she taught him to 'take off his tie in public', how to manipulate the *descamisados* (the unshirted poor). Then, knowing how despised she was by the Anglophile establishment, she threw herself into a cause, the relief of the same suffering and injustice she had once known.

Fantastically lifted above the gutter, she communicated directly with the people who were stuck there. She threw gifts down to them with one hand. No one knows how much she kept in her other for herself. Whether her popular canonization identified sanctity and whose cause it was she served still divides Argentinians along political lines. Was Peron a fascist or a liberator of the poor? Her philanthropy built a thousand schools and a hundred hospitals, but what did she get out of it? In virtue, motive matters. The musical merely ponders her relationship to the cult she became in her short life. She is famous because she is famous. Her life had the duration of a shooting star and very early she disappeared into the stardom, the image that people formed of her, into what people *wanted* to believe about her. So a metaphysical question lingers after her, one that in her driven, ever insecure ambition she possibly never thought about: who *really* was she?

Rome decided not to answer this question. It ignored a huge flood of demands for canonization that followed her death from cancer at the age of 33. Someone in Rome always seems to know the wisdom of doing nothing. Nevertheless, until the death of Pope John Paul II, Eva's was the biggest funeral in history – 1 million on the day and 3 million mourners filing past her coffin.

We don't know so much about San Miniato. An Armenian prince (perhaps), he was beheaded during the Decian persecution. Nonplussed, he promptly picked up his head (no perhaps about it), then walked up the hill to lie down and become the patronal relic above which one of the world's most beautiful churches (and Michelangelo's favourite), now an Olivetan Benedictine monastery, has arisen. We don't know his motives or even if he was historical enough to have any. But in his saintly afterlife he built a church that not only pulls Florentines up the same hill every evening to watch the sun set over this city of beauty, it is also made from stone and marble a place where the spiritual becomes *sensible*. The Romanesque harmonies of the architecture and the musical silence of the geometrical patterns, which cover the church inside and out like tasteful tattoos, cast a benevolent spell. It houses a deeper and more interior beauty than outside in the bright sunlight from which you entered the coolness of the dark church. It bestows on even the most tired tourist a momentary reverence and silence.

San Miniato did much better in his final resting place than Eva. She lies now in a small family mausoleum in the chic, crowded Recoleta cemetery, among the patricians who hated her rather than with the poor who worshipped her. Three years after her death, while Peron was planning a memorial to her as large as the Statue of Liberty, a coup toppled him. For reasons that medieval monks would have understood, Eva's body was snatched by the new government. They feared it becoming a totem around which opposition could form, but they also felt uneasy about possessing it. Argentinians, in the opinion of their fellow South Americans, think of themselves as displaced Europeans and the farcical fate of Eva's relics may illustrate this. The body was moved from one minder to another, at one point spending several days in a military van in a Buenos Aires side street. Then it disappeared, was traced to Bonn but instantly translocated to Milan where the Italians, who understand what relics mean, buried it until Peron regained power and it returned home.

San Miniato, whoever he is, is seen to be saint *and* martyr. Eva is still working at convincing history that she is saint not charlatan. Should we conclude that this shows the need for a canonical procedure to prove holiness? When one sees how political canonization can be, one wonders. Holiness is one thing, sanctity in the eyes of the world is another. The holy do not need a certificate to prove it. Celebrity – religious or the kind Hollywood makes – is short-lived. Stardom, like the cult of saints revolves – though in different ways – around bodies, before or after death, and bodies are famously mortal.

So how can we tell who is truly good? Is it all fantasy and projection – the worship of saints or stars? In the dark spellbound crypt of San Miniato, thinking of Evita, I concluded that there is a way to gauge the authenticity of a life. Not fame, but the waves of good, emanating from it down the centuries and becoming visible in many forms of beauty.

July 2005

9

Paradise with Serpents

I once met a really rich poor man on a beach in Mexico. I was walking through the warm surf, watching the sun sink into the horizon in a golden glory and the birds swooping on the unsuspecting fish that swim in large numbers to shore in the evening. A few men, young and old, were fishing in the abundance from the shore. Some cast nets and brought in catches of evangelical proportions. Others used single lines. One was reeling in a large fish as we walked by and we congratulated him. As happens easily when work is not stressful and the environment is conducive, we stopped awhile and talked, satisfying a natural curiosity about each other. Where we lived and what we were doing with the gift of life on this strangely beautiful earth.

Oscar is a fisherman in Guerrero, the poorest state of Mexico. His place of work, a coastline that would make a developer drool, is still untouched by big capitalism. Oscar gets about 60 pesos for each fish and on a good evening the sea blesses him with eight of them. In a country where the average income might be 80 pesos (about £3.50) a day, he was a rich man, with just a little more than enough. His wealth was not merely economic. His overheads were low; his commute easy; his working conditions paradisiacal. And he had the inner glow that becomes visible in people who work collaboratively with other creatures within the bounds of nature rather than exploiting it. But he was busy and had more fish to catch, so I couldn't satisfy all my curiosity. No doubt, like all of us he had family problems, health anxieties and even some unrealizable dreams. But does happiness mean having no problems. Or seeing them in perspective?

Many people go into marriages or monasteries in search of paradise because they have had a glimpse of Eden. But every paradise is full of serpents, our own and others' egos. Before long they crawl out of the undergrowth. The disillusionment they cause makes for much marital (or monastic) sadness and bitterness. Perhaps it is only then, though, that the Kingdom of God begins to make sense as something different from a commercial paradise or a mythical Eden. Luxury resorts attract the unsatisfied and can make them more so. Myths are hard to distinguish from fantasies. The Kingdom by contrast is not about places but people. It is about relationships that reveal compassion and forgiveness as the real values underlying happiness and producing peace sustained by the love of justice.

Mexico is a paradise with many rampant serpents. Corruption is endemic. A small hotel owner whom I met with during the retreat told me how he had caught an employee stealing. The owner called him in, presented the evidence and told him to leave. The employee simply refused. He was the brother of a local police-man, he said – that said a lot. If the owner insisted then he, the employee, would wait one night to rape and kill the owner's wife. So the employer had to wait and give him assignments with fewer pickings. Gradually he would ease this particular serpent out into a neighbour's garden.

Yet there is rampant honesty too. It is different from the big law-abiding brother to the north. In the USA, if you are white and middle class, you can generally trust a cop. Financial and polit-ical corruption are on a bigger scale and more easily wriggle off the legal hook. In Catholic Mexico, sin is accepted everywhere. No one denies that serpents do often rule or that the poorest people are their most frequent victims. There is not the hypocrisy of the northern puritan maintaining the image of freedom and fairness. Hard-working Mexicans working in the USA send $22 billion back to their families each year. This is more than the revenue the country earns from either of its biggest industries, oil and tourism. They do the most menial jobs in California and the south-western states, which still wish to deny these workers medical care or education for their children.

The hotel owner I met told me of his plan to start a school for poor children – good food, the children's mothers employed at the school so they too can learn domestic skills, how to use computers, and English. Above all he wants to train them in the virtues of honesty and good citizenship so as to protect them from the venom of violence. As he described his vision I heard the Kingdom.

When I left the country after the retreat, there was a long line and much chaos at the airport. The passenger in front of me, a rich gringo in Hawaii shorts, was red in the face. A box containing some frozen fish that he was checking in was overweight. He was remonstrating unpleasantly with the Mexican agent who was courteously and patiently explaining the regulations. He was conciliatory, offering to open the box and help him remove some of the contents until it could meet the requirements. The passenger sneered at this. In a deliberately audible aside to his companion he accused the agent of trying to steal his fish (maybe one of Oscar's). The desk agent and I and most of those watching this tantrum winced and waited.

I wouldn't have been surprised to see the agent leap over the counter and throttle him. But he swallowed the insult and looked calmly at the passenger with self-control and dignity. Not for the first time on this trip I glimpsed the Kingdom, this time in the grace of non-violence.

February 2006

10

Dediri

Mick Lowcock, the parish priest of Mount Isa for more than 20 years, was driving me around the town after our very early morning meditation. In the cool new light of the day he slowed down beside the dry and dusty river bed. A group of men sat in the middle, as still and silent as meditators in a circle. Fr Mick's outback toughness melted. He smiled and sent a kindly greeting over the dust. They slowly looked up and sent a heavy, sad response back through their alcoholic stupor.

Mount Isa is an isolated mining town in Northern Queensland in the diocese of Townsville, which is about the size of Britain. The outback stretches silently in every direction. Remote as it is, it is also full of unexpected connections to the wider world. (Coincidentally one of our recent UK co-ordinators was born there.) The night before I had spoken in Fr Mick Lowcock's parish church and met the Aboriginal Australian who had represented his people in a UN conference on indigenous peoples. He was an articulate and urbane man. Amos, who came over without embarrassment to join our conversation, was a rougher diamond, more like one of the men on the river bed that morning.

One day I spoke to a hundred Catholic teachers from this part of the diocese. For the past two years it has been part of the 'Coming Home' programme of the Catholic Education Office, introducing meditation to children in all grades. The seminar was held in the Irish Club, something between a leisure centre, a pub and a casino. I arrived with Bishop Michael Putney (who was co-chair of the global Catholic–Methodist dialogue). As we walked to the meeting room past lines of the profitably addictive pokie machines, one-armed bandits, I said to Bishop Putney that this felt like real Catholicism – speaking on contemplation in an Irish casino deep in the Australian bush.

The deepest and most silent of all the surprising connections here in this desert is with the land itself. At every event in Australia now the participants are 'welcomed' to the land on which it is happening by a representative of its original tribal owners. Today as elsewhere it seemed more than a politically correct, liberal gesture. It is an attempt to bridge the unbridgeable. Many Australians have now accepted themselves as newcomers to the planet's oldest continent and some grieve at the irreversible damage done to the native peoples over the past two centuries. Until a few decades ago, a white farmer could get a police permit to shoot Aboriginal 'trespassers' on 'his' land; and not much would happen if he neglected to obtain it. Despite the devastation of their culture, there are good leaders among the indigenous people, who are supported by people like Fr Mick and Bishop Putney. But the majority are more like the drunks waking up on the dry river bed, a lost human tribe only half-struggling to transmit their ancient wisdom before it is forgotten.

The Church has been part of this awakening to historical responsibility and it has been blessed by the broken people it is now caring for. From them Christians are learning of *dediri*, the contemplative spirituality of a people with an ancestral memory of 40,000 years. The alcoholics on the river bed might not be benefiting from it, but the wisdom is being transmitted by some of their elders to whites whom they recognize as able to listen and understand the stories that carry their tradition. One Catholic teacher, predisposed by his meditation practice, was invited to undergo initiation into the local tribe because, after observing him for a long time, they saw both a capacity to understand their knowledge and the discretion to respect their secrets.

Dediri is a deep, silent, non-questioning listening to the land and its inhabitants. It takes time and attention. As they witness the constant, environmental wounding of their terrestrial 'guardians', the Aborigines can see what is happening. Like most of us, they feel helpless as the global insanity of self-mutation continues, as the rains fail, the ice cover melts and the deforested lands flood. With a surprising lack of bitterness they share, like other indigenous peoples, a healing wisdom with those who care to listen. In this there is another connection to find here, that between the old and new wisdom. One Christian Aborigine came up to me after a talk on meditation where I had spoken of the long tradition of Christian meditation. She explained how her people had essentially known this wisdom for much longer but also how her new faith had shown her what her people had been listening to these 40 millennia: the Word of God sounding at the heart of creation.

Two days later, beaming and mitred, Bishop Putney and the Archbishop of Brisbane, the Apostolic Nuncio to Australia and a long line of priests waited patiently outside before entering the newly refurbished cathedral of Townsville. The indigenous people in traditional undress were 'smoking' the building, readying it for its re-consecration. It was a connecting moment, as the traditional owners welcomed the newcomers who, with all their past sins, had shared the new faith with them. In Sydney, people might think they are closer to the centre of wealth and fashion than here in Townsville. But through the liturgy that evening I thought the centre of the world is where you make it, if there is sufficient *dediri* in you to know that the centre is where God is.

A girl about to graduate from high school recently told me that high on the list of the 30 things she was asked to identify as her life goals was 'to be a local'. It struck me as a rather poignant ambition that illustrated how rootless the globalized subculture can make us feel. We can communicate instantly anywhere and yet often feel that we belong nowhere. The Aboriginal people here once knew that they belonged to the land. The newcomers proved them wrong and said 'the land belongs to us'. Yet the young girl's hope carries an important intuition. If enough people felt it, it might connect the local alcoholics on the dry river bed to the multinationals and to the deracinated city-dwellers everywhere, a bridge of compassion and concern. Perhaps isolated parish churches and restored cathedrals can teach us to learn how to be locals wherever we are on this earth, before we forget what 'being a local' really means.

June 2006

11

Jailbird

Security clearance takes weeks. The visiting rules are quirky and strictly enforced, like not wearing sandals without a back-strap. When you arrive at Corcoran Federal Penitentiary in California, you wonder why anyone would willingly come here and how the unwilling are challenged to their core. The inmate I had come to receive as an oblate of our community told me about his arrival. He and his fellow prisoners were pulled out of the transport van and made to wait for some minutes under the ruthless sun. They looked in silence at the bleak place they had been committed to for a minimum of ten years. His companion broke the silence: 'You know, I'm really going to change my travel agent.'

The prison sits in the desert, a place so inhuman in appearance and inhumane in conception that it feels extra-terrestrial, a residence for aliens. In the earliest human buildings, about 5,000 years ago, you find decorative detail. Nothing here mars the lifeless impersonality of the prison buildings, no glimmer of playfulness or aesthetic pleasure. The aim is total control and suppression of individuality. It is an impossible aim. You cannot control people in this way but you can deform them. As you drive towards it over the desert you see the cold logical quadrangles of razor wire, the look-out towers, the squat buildings with the outward-facing windows painted over. The human cost of American security, punishing the bad, the repressed nightmare that protects the desperate dream of the Californian good life.

Yet if art doesn't redeem it, nature tries. Another kind of jailbird has built a nest in the wire at the top of the inner gate. Three of the Kingsburg meditation group, who lead the group in the prison, look up with me at the defiance of nature against the unnatural, this tender thing in this wholly ungreen place. Where art is denied, religion tries too. Sr Carolyn is the only Catholic chaplain for 12,000 inmates. There are also two Protestants and one half-time Muslim and Jewish chaplains respectively struggling against shrinking budgets. Sr Carolyn is elderly, overweight and walks with difficulty, so I drive her in the golf cart to the chapel along bare right-angled roads. I think of the camp at Belsen. Like the bird, she quietly defies the inhumanity and tries to build a spiritual nest for these brutalized, sometimes brutal men who return her love.

At the chapel a group of about 30 inmates are arriving, each carrying a deep pain but chatting and laughing. We have two hours together. First, I meet Russ with whom I have been corresponding for some time and who will become a Benedictine oblate novice of our community today. Oblates are people who live in the spirit of the Rule of St Benedict in the circumstances of their own lives. Usually they are attached to a physical monastery but with us they *are* the community of a 'monastery without walls'. Russ will live the Benedictine precepts of stability, conversion and obedience in this place. He has a healthy sense of irony and we laugh at the meanings of stability and obedience – and of walls – in Corcoran. He is about 35, well educated, observant and funny.

When I commiserate about the hardships of life in prison he stops me. Not so bad, he says. He keeps clear of the bad guys and the mean guards 'who had their candy stolen from them when they were kids'. I had seen some of the bad guys as we came in, tattooed, muscular honchos who strut around the yard with their bodyguards and minions in tow. Some run their outside drug businesses from prison, control the corrupt guards and abuse the weaker men. But Russ told his mother, 'There are 6 billion people in the world. It's highly unlikely I'm the worst off.'

'I was in prison and you visited me.' You have to go into a prison to know what Jesus means and why this is one of the corporal works of mercy. When the group was gathered we did some *lectio* on a shared gospel story. Nearly everyone participated. The silent ones were paying attention. I felt their painful joy, the inner light visible in this dark place, many of the signs of contemplation. They had a confident, steady gaze. They listened to each other and had quick humour. They seemed gentle with each other. I thought what a good community meeting you could have with them. People would speak their mind, not be scared to express themselves but murmur afterwards.

Prison is one of the places I feel the Kingdom of God most immediately. Here, and in other marginal situations, this experience of presence and the freedom of love seems closer than in religious settings where the God-talk fails to bring God down to earth. Then we sang a song and meditated in perfect silence for half an hour. When the seventh seal was opened 'there was silence in heaven for the space of half an hour'. The silence that is so rare in church.

Another song and discussion, and then Russ was received as a novice. Some of his friends remained and saw him receive the Rule and medal of St Benedict and sign his chart. He spoke to them of what this meant for him: a sense of transcendence and community in a world where the personal and the communal are so often stifled. We walked out into the sun-baked yard, past the gangs and the unsmiling guards, like a nightmare playground that would have been a setting for one of Dante's circles of the Inferno.

Everything was set up to expect the worst in human nature. I said goodbye to Russ, who smiled beatifically, full of the grace of the moment. As we left, Sr Carolyn took me to meet the captain of the guard. He was an imposing Rambo figure, dripping with armoury. But he had made some concessions for our visit and we wanted to thank him. He was, as you might expect, a guarded personality but listened as I spoke about the goodness I felt in the men

I met. He didn't dismiss it entirely but nodded and said that it was true, there was goodness in them, but 'don't forget you see the best in them'. He was right, but that is not such a bad thing to see.

Prison is the mirror image of a monastery, just as a totalitarian institution is what René Girard calls the 'monstrous double' of the Church. The worst happens when the people in power try to control everything. Eventually they fail, but the lust for uniformity and dominion always revives. Power is the great temptation of the Church, too, and when it succumbs it is renewed from the margins by the saints and mystics.

'The sparrow herself builds a nest for her brood by your altars.' The verse of the psalm popped into my mind as we left the compound and walked again under the bird's nest on top of the wire. The holy makes strange appearances, often funny and unpredictable. Mysterious, too, like Russ following the gentle Rule of St Benedict in such an unforgiving place.

May 2004

12

The Rolling Stone

So, who moved the stone? Three Gospels say it was 'rolled away', John that it was 'moved away'. Three say it had happened by the time Mary of Magdala reached the tomb. Matthew somewhat stretches our literal credulity by actually describing it being rolled away. This is achieved by a (presumably muscular) angel who descends in front of the two Marys and the guards, with a face like lightning and clothes white as snow. He then sits on the stone as the guards shake with fear and lie like the dead.

Well, the modern reader says, what are the facts? Several highly strung female witnesses, an empty tomb – and the rolled-away stone. A scattered group of fearful male disciples. And the mother of Jesus and the other women who, as always, held the group together until they recovered their evangelical zeal. A new age began to dawn on that Sunday morning about which we have such different accounts. Is there one explanation that fits them all? There are certainly many reasonable objections. A contemptuous Roman writer, who thought that the Christian sect could not be taken seriously as it was neither a religion nor a philosophy, asked an uncomfortable question for the prosecution. If Jesus had in fact risen from the dead – that is, if it was not just a new version of a familiar myth – why didn't he appear to Pilate, the High Priest, his executioners and critics and confound them all? That would have put an end to the matter. And it would have been sweet revenge and convinced everyone.

There's still the stone. If, in his subtle body, Jesus could move through doors and appear at will, why move the stone? To make it easier for the women to see he wasn't there? What does it all mean? At what level can we verify its truth? Can we be certain? Wittgenstein believed it was possible with intellectual integrity to transcend scepticism and achieve certainty, though it's not easy to follow his reasoning. About the resurrection he has this to say:

> But if I am to be *really* saved – what I need is certainty – not wisdom, dreams or speculation – and this certainty is faith. And faith is faith in what is needed by my heart, my soul, not my speculative intelligence. Perhaps we can say: Only love can believe the Resurrection. Or: It is love that believes the Resurrection. (*Culture and Value*, Wiley-Blackwell, 2nd edn, 1998)

After a Christian has celebrated enough Easters, the contentious arguments lose their interest. One learns by entering the mystery being revealed in the telling of the story among those who sit through the Triduum and feel the wonder at what is being retold. The rational mind can still wrestle with all these questions. But one comes closer to the answer – love as Wittgenstein says – by letting the religious imagination work on the story. The heart opened by faith and surprised by joy sees the rightness of the story by finding it within the story of our own life. Whatever happened early on that Sunday morning when the new age dawned we can never describe; but the rolled-away stone is in us. Telling the story is part of discovering this inner meaning.

Loquacious taxi drivers are full of stories repeated to their captive audience. As well as the women, they would have been a good choice to carry the good news.

I tried to avoid eye contact in the rear-view mirror with Matt driving me to Belfast airport one foggy morning as I was more concerned that he kept his eye on the road. But his stories of the Troubles were fascinating. He told me how many taxi drivers had been shot in their most dangerous of professions; and how he had once mistakenly been pushed up against a wall in a dark alley until the person they were hunting down drove up and had their guns turned on him. Throughout the hour he spoke at me he never mentioned the words Catholic or Protestant, Republican or Loyalist. He was sick of it all. The politicians getting paid, with big perks, and often not even turning up to work at Stormont; the £7.7 billion annual subsidy to a province the size of Birmingham; the absurdity of the Troubles being the biggest employer. 'It's cloud cuckoo land, here,' he kept saying in his thick Ulster accent.

I was struck by what echoed through his opinionated eloquence, from the soul of this oddly lovable lost tribe. I had heard the same once from a professional Northern Ireland mediator who told me how indulged they were in this small province compared with other ravaged parts of the world like the Balkans or Rwanda, whose conflicts had been far more devastating. What I heard was not self-hatred but a new self-awareness, the ability to rise above oneself and one's culture. It was touched with the rhetoric and humour of the island but it showed the signs of transcendence.

What had rolled away this ancient stone of sectarian self-obsession? When exactly had it happened? The combatants still can't agree on much and don't like each other much more, but that a big stone has rolled they will all acknowledge. Many are still weeping, looking into an empty tomb, which is a dark and bleak place. But some might already have caught sight of a fresh-looking young gardener who seems vaguely familiar.

The end of the Troubles, like the resurrection, is a new beginning. It takes time for it to sink in that a corner has been turned and the old patterns have dissolved. But there *is* a good story to tell. Not a headline with an exclusive photograph, but a rolling away of despair. The original stone must have been as heavy as all the other stones in history that ever blocked life. It is still moving, still gathering momentum. We slowly understand that the stone is our own.

April 2006

13

The Fall

As a native of a small, congested, tarmacked and irritable island, the great spaces of the Americas have always been a relief and a source of revelation, places to breathe in and see a further horizon. During the autumn in eastern Canada the edges of the wilderness become almost vulgarly beautiful as the trees turn into vast stretches of scarlet, chrome yellows, dark gold and rich brown. Mountain after mountain the cry of autumn becomes a chorus, like a demonstration for some passionate but unspoken cause. They are going out in glory, making a last desperate statement against the coming death, an appeal to beauty as truth, before the arctic winds and frosts strip and push them into a long white silence of winter. During the summer you take leaves for granted, but in their dying you pay attention to details. And then, just as the dying can love every moment of life, so the more you watch the more you want to see.

In Nova Scotia I first heard of 'Seton Watching', a method of being in nature attributed to the British naturalist Ernest Thompson Seton, who was a pioneer of animal fiction as well as the founder of the Boy Scouts in the United States. In the 1880s he came to Canada from his native Durham and soon formed a life-long love for forests and wilderness and a passion for wolves. As an educator, Black Wolf, as he called himself, would take young people out of town and sit them completely still in the woods for 20 minutes, for nothing but an intense watching and listening. The stillness attracted the wild animals to approach, and the listeners became, through watching, part of the natural surroundings. 'In the wood the silent watcher sees the most,' he wrote in *Birch Bark Roll of the Woodcraft Indians*, and added, less contemplatively, 'The great difficulty in watching is how to pass the time.'

In Quebec I was passing the time quite easily watching the drama of the autumn colours evolve to some sudden climax I didn't want to miss. The woods were in suspense even though the end of the performance was obvious. It would be the same as every year. The glory of this world would fade and the branches would be bare. I was in my room in the retreat centre as two friends who were on the retreat passed by my window, walking in the easy silence of their long marriage along the path that led into the woods. They had just told me that the good news they had celebrated with me a few months ago – she did *not* have Parkinsons – had been cruelly reversed. The tests had been redone as the symptoms increased; and now she did have it. They had begun to study the disease. The decline was becoming, like the changing colours, irreversible.

The dying of the leaves attracts attention. As they die, the green pigmented chlorophyll decays rapidly. Yellow carotenids also break down, but more slowly, and red anthocyanins are added as new short-lived creations of the dying process. So the familiar green of the leaves dissolves to reveal the yellow beneath, and then the reds and browns and golds are squeezed out as well. The lurid beauty was there all along, but hidden behind the mundane. It is the shortening days of the year, the abbreviation of the light, that force the trees to prepare like this for their winter sleep.

My friends were wrapped up defiantly against the first cold fingers of the Canadian winter. They walked slowly arm in arm, he a little shorter than she, into the woods, into the colours. Rumi said that the lover of God should pray to be coloured with the col- our of God. When we had spoken with tears about the medical news and the timeline, they seemed like two castaways. Blessedly together, at least, but nonetheless being separated and singled out. They were childlike, surprised and somewhat indignant by the new twist of fate, helpless yet learning to adapt to a new phase of their life. A wilderness of solitude was moving closer to them on all sides opening up a new sense of who and where they were. They were getting to understand this new landscape simply by being in it. God's inexpressible colour was becoming stronger in them. There could be no resistance. They would have to watch the colours play out and wait for the leaves to fall. At mass after sunset we all prayed with them, anointing and blessing them for the season of their lives they had moved into. If faith in face of mortality has colour it is like the glorious autumn palette of Canada.

In a few weeks there will be fewer leaves on the trees than when I wrote this piece. Every fallen leaf has left a scar on the stem it once clung to. Next to the scar of its loss is already a tiny bud from which new shoots and leaves will spring.

October 2006

14

Great Silence

It may have been the sudden shift from London into the slowness of the film or the dinner just before going into the cinema, but I dozed through the first half-hour of *Into Great Silence*, the three-hour-long portrayal of life in the Carthusian solitude of La Grande Chartreuse. Like the crowds who have flocked to it around secular Europe, making it an unexpected and bizarre success, I was drawn by the enthusiastic reviews and several invitations to see for myself how a film without a plot – that was not even about bird migration or penguins but the most enclosed of Christian monks – could have touched the nerve of a culture as insensitive to traditional religion and as sensation-driven as ours.

Seventeen years before it was made the director had approached the abbot to ask permission to live in the monastery and film the life. He didn't receive a downright refusal but was told they were not yet ready. Fifteen years later the abbot called him to say they were now ready. I don't know the reason for the abbot's decision but I admire his sense of timing. His community was indeed ready to bear witness with irresistible innocence to the enigma of contemplative life and the peculiar way it is lived in monasteries. The camera is like an unjudging eye. It sees and yet there is no comment. It is not a documentary nor a promotion of the life-choice.

In one section, the camera sits in the solitude of a young monk's austere cell watching but seemingly not intruding on his prayer cycles, the 15-minute sessions on knees and up, his spiritual reading, his seriously concentrated eating. As viewers of this privacy we are made to feel the awkward intimacy of the prime medium of our age, the voyeurism of its objectifying eye, the big-brotherhood of the way it makes the mundane so engrossing. The film moves as slowly as the life of its subjects. Like the monks, it makes no effort to justify its existence. There are no stars. No dramas. No vocational crises. No lament for the path not taken. It is difficult to say whether or not it has a tinge of romanticism. Perhaps anything that appears complete makes us feel nostalgic. What it omits seems not to exist, not to be concealed. What is revealed is a sparkling emptiness.

The only uneasy moment in the film is a formal community recreation period, but ask any novice and he will tell you these can be the most difficult of all monastic moments. The romp and sliding in the snow on the community outing seems genuinely boyish and, filmed from a distance, it makes the solitude of their life appear all the more cosmic, like a plantation of chosen human-ity on a spaceship heading on a long voyage, with nothing to do, to a new planet. At generous intervals there are living cinematic portraits of the monks who stare silently, with strange ease, into the lens. The faces are young and eager, old and tired, intelligent and a little stupid. There is no judgement, no favouritism. They are as the life is. At the end of the film come the only words, when an old blind monk says how his loss of sight has helped him see God better.

At first I thought the film became so popular because it illus-trates an alternative and strange lifestyle. Unless they have chosen to die, which happens, monasteries are usually looking or hoping for vocations. But Carthusian life is rarely if ever represented at vocation exhibitions. It is a very unusual form of a very unusual life. But for many people today their unsatisfactory lifestyles and the sense of horror at our self-harming behaviour suggest an entrap-ment, a loss of freedom in a world of infinite choice. Here one sees something utterly different. It may not attract many candidates but it shows we do have freedom and we can use it for happiness.

Second, what is being portrayed is perhaps the only kind of religious experience widely felt to be authentic today. Without proclaimed dogma and yet built on faith and belief, not seeking recognition or converts, not moralizing or judging, the life of this monastery – at least as it is shown in this film – has a primal *isness*. Maybe today, as in many earlier periods of social crisis and religious turmoil, it is solitude and silence that appear salvifically on the radar screen of the culture. The solitary and silent life – alone together – witnesses most eloquently to the universal nature of the God whom everyone else is claiming as their own.

Third, it is about more than religion. It is a love story. This is the secret of the film. The monks seem happy but are not in love with each other. If they love each other it is because they are in love with the same invisible yet apparently ever-present person. Unnamed, unseen, even unspoken to, God plays in every scene. At first, one assumes it is the visible actors who are the lovers. Slowly it dawns that they are mirrors. The love we speak of is not our love for God but God's love for us.

February 2007

15

The Siege of Sarajevo

There are so many stories, atrocities, scandals, so much outrage and anger and so many demands on our sympathy, that opting out of the News is an understandable choice. The newsmakers also encourage this when it becomes entertainment or sensational reconstruction. It takes filters to stay in the loop of the global village while continuing to see the wood for the trees. With so much embedded brainwashing, how do we maintain our criteria for evaluating, forming informed views and yet staying both detached and concerned? We have to stay in touch. Only genuine hermits, because they are in touch with all, have the right to stay outside the fray.

But, better than watching the News is to see the places and people of history for oneself, even years after they have slipped into media archives. Take Sarajevo, for example. I can remember reading the news and seeing pictures of the constant shelling. I felt shocked at the news of the ethnic cleansing, deportations, torture, rapes and the massacre at Srebrenica that showed that the madness that infected Europe once can have a resurgence. The Bosnian war, however, was in a corner of Europe that I knew only through history textbooks and 'eastern European' acquaintances. The problem is one of trust. The News is selected by journalists who choose what they think will amuse, shock or titillate – and sell. Today a tragedy is headline, tomorrow it's page 12. Reading of the International Court of Justice distinguishing finely between 'genocide' and 'acts of genocide', the words made reality an abstraction. For four years Sarajevo became news on the front page and in cartoons, but not every day. It depended what else there was to make the News new. Yet each day, for its inhabitants, it must have seemed like an eternal apocalypse The siege of Sarajevo from 5 August 1992 to 29 February 1996 was the longest in modern warfare.

It is an old, idiosyncratic city of complex charm, mosques and churches and, after the Holocaust, one remaining synagogue with the records of the Holocaust deportations. With a culture that made it the Muslim intellectual capital of Europe, Sarajevo accommodated Muslim, Orthodox, Catholic and Jewish citizens. Its markets and short bridges are bustling again, but during the siege, when 12,000 of its inhabitants were killed and 50,000 mutilated, a daily average of 329 artillery shells fell. The peak was 3,771 on 21 July 1993. (I might have been on holiday that day or giving a retreat in some peaceful monastery.) The city is surrounded by hills where the Serbian nationalist forces took up positions like the Greeks at Troy, fanatically trying to destroy the newly independent Bosnia-Herzegovnia. 'Christians' insane with merciless hatred. Sarajevo Serbs who refused to oppress the Muslims were themselves executed. In the 'sniper alleys' people were picked off as they stood in conversation on a street corner. Soccer matches, water-gatherers, bread queues, the deliberate destruction of one of the world's greatest collections of Oriental manuscripts. This happened in a city that in 1984 hosted the Winter Olympics. It was a city of scholars, artists and conservatoires, Franciscans and Sufis.

Maybe at times one has to deny horror in order to stay sane. If so, one should distinguish between repression – the denial of a painful reality – and suppression – the conscious laying aside of the past for a better future. The past is suppressed in the new Sarajevo, not forgotten, and its surviving memories are strangely seeds of hope.

Now that it's 'history', the new leaders try to control how it is recorded. The religious leaders say they are looking ahead. But the passion and pain of their memories soon surface in any conversation. They say that it is encouraging that now there is no violence, but this is not so with the post-war demographic changes that took place. There are few Orthodox Christians left in Sarajevo. Exactly how many there are of any religious or ethnic group is a political fact no one really wants to talk about. Maybe it's better not to count. Even the suggestion of a census is politically dangerous. It *is* surprising and wonderfully consoling, though, to see the readiness for inter-religious dialogue and prayer. But then, as one Muslim leader told me, 'We know only too well what happens when dialogue stops.'

If all cities have karmas – like Jerusalem or Rome – Sarajevo has its karma and seeks its place in a new history. Its citizens tell you, almost with pride, that it was the place where the first European war of the twentieth century began with the assassination of the Archduke Ferdinand and where the century's last war, the Bosnian war, ended. We find meaning where we can.

The worst period of its history also makes it a place where lessons of civic virtue can be learned, ways of peace-building can be developed and dialogue practised. Where inhumanity once reigned it can also be redeemed. In such places where so much blood has been shed there is also often a pregnant silence with seeds of the hope of being fully human that we must continuously relearn.

August 2007

16

The Sea Monster

It was a hot evening barely cooled by the sea breeze. For the whole day an old-fashioned summer had ignored climactic change. It was the equinox of childhoods when night and day are magically the same length and the sun crosses the celestial equator with a declination of zero degrees.

Bere Island is composed of an inhabited area facing the shore, and a pure wilderness facing the Atlantic. The wilderness may not be huge in terms of square miles but at times it feels as immense as the desert or the tundra. After a few hours clambering through the wilderness and then along the crumbling edges of the cliffs, I was exhilaratingly exhausted. Physical exertion is the quickest way to a feeling of achievement. I was sweaty and scratched by brambles and looking forward to the blessings of civilization, especially a cup of tea and a shower before vespers and meditation. However, as I came in view of human habitation, on the edge of middle earth, adventure beckoned. Where the narrow path emerged along the water's edge and offered to lead me to level ground and the comforts of home, a strange sound reached me, unidentifiable and yet oddly intimate. Carried on the wind from the sea, it was not a voice but had a human intensity. I wanted to get home but I could not refuse this summons.

So, I slid down one side of the land's edge towards the sea, glad of my hiking boots. It was not high here but slippery and hard to keep balance. The sound became stronger as I descended. By its rhythmic pulsation I felt sure it was more than the product of wind, water and rock. It seemed sentient.

I came as close as I could to where the source seemed to be. The two sides of the cliff converged sharply in a cleft in the pock-marked rock. They almost touched. But in the narrow gap between them there was an opening into a thin, deep chasm where the sea respired, flooding in and emptying out. 'The moving waters at their priestlike task, Of pure ablution round earth's human shores', as Keats described it.

It was a wild kind of liturgy here at the edge of Christendom. Deep down and way back, in a dark space, a small chamber held the secret of the cry. As I listened there was no doubt it was breathing agitatedly; its respiration was related to the tidal surge. When the sea flooded in, it must be causing pain to some imprisoned creature. Often it thrashed around in a desperate attempt to escape, then fell back exhausted. I couldn't see it but I could hear and feel its suffering presence.

I was not sure if the creature trapped in the cavern was dangerous but I was glad that as the aperture was so narrow I had no option to enter it. At times its protest against its unyielding environment sounded so poignant as to be crying 'save me!' Isn't this when we are meant to intervene in the natural world? Not to stop a hawk attacking newborn lambs and extracting their eyes but rescuing a fellow creature in distress or protecting its species from extinction. Is this not the difference humans are meant to make to the world? Humans can be as self-sacrificing for other creatures as they are (at times) for each other, helping other beings without counting the cost to their own comfort or survival. Yet it seemed a highly dangerous project to go into the cavern. So desperate were the cries that it might be impossible to pull the creature out – seal, dolphin or a small whale perhaps, even a less familiar creature of the deep. I left for tea.

That night I dreamed of Grendel, the first monster that Beowulf slew because it was terrorizing his people. Grendel, a descendant of the race of Cain, has one of its arms cut off by the hero. But the battle was not over. Mortally wounded, it returns to its cave, and its mother, not as strong as Grendel but, impassioned by revenge, comes by night to the hall where the feast for Beowulf has just ended. She retrieves Grendel's arm that Beowulf had taken as a trophy and returns to her underwater cave. Beowulf goes in pursuit and is attacked as he reaches the cave and barely survives. Finding a magic sword, he dispatches her and wins glory. But soon after this, in a battle with a *wyrm*, a dragon that an escaped slave had awakened by stealing a cup from his lair, Beowulf himself was mortally wounded.

Fragments of these tales filled my dream world that night. During the day, in conscious life, the trapped creature did not seem mythical, any more than logistical meetings in the Pentagon to discuss military action seem to repeat ancient patterns of the past. Reason and metrics are the basis of science. We assume that they inform our decision making more than our unconscious fears and addictions. Maybe, though, everything is mythical except the pure truth. Myth mediates the truth but *is* an intermediary. If it is not there in the contemplative clear light of day – when thoughts and fancy have been laid aside – it was not real. Cain's race loves battles and adventures, exalts dead heroes, ignores its armless or legless warriors when they are brought home. We repeat the past in new ways with better technology. The Master's saying, that whoever lives by the sword will perish by it, spoils the adventure.

I spoke about the trapped creature to some men on the island. They were non-committal. I said I would return to the spot to see if it was still there and maybe we could talk about a rescue party. Their guarded reaction was the beginning of a new perspective. When I got to the cave the wailing sound of pain was still there. As rhythmic as before, and quite obviously synchronized with the respiration of the sea.

July 2007

17

Henry Cook

Henry Cook worked his whole life as a farm labourer in a village near Sudbury in Suffolk, a very English county in East Anglia. One autumn day, as a young man, he lost his right hand during the threshing. He bravely continued working, but some years later lost his other arm in a similar accident. For the rest of his life he made do with no hands and barely half of one arm. There were no artificial limbs on the NHS in those days, so he rigged up a leather strap held round his neck with string. This enabled him both the dignity and conviviality of continuing to work in other tasks, as well as holding his own in the pub. He would deftly lift his pint mug with his teeth and push it up to his mouth with his stump. Never married, he died in the Sudbury workhouse about 80 years ago. He was never known to complain about his lot and remained cheerful and active in the community that reared him and never excluded him. He achieved nothing of historical importance except a place in the collective memory of the people of his local area, a presence passed on in the ancient rituals of storytelling.

One cold Sunday night in Lent the Sudbury theatre was, as usual, full for one of its local history evenings. Seats are sold out weeks in advance for people to listen to short talks from passionate amateur historians: the mystery of the 'lost village' that died out in the fifteenth century, the Black Death in Suffolk, an old bus service called Corona Coaches, lawyering in Sudbury in the nineteenth century or field-name clues to the Dark Ages. And, that evening, the talk on Henry Cook which held the audience spellbound.

It was a secular liturgy. People chose to gather in virtue of their shared identity. They enjoyed reciting the stories that made them who they are. They felt enriched and enhanced by what they learned and shared. After the talks everyone joined in an open discussion, adding their own memories or corrections to those of others. As liturgy it was very low church. There was no priesthood except that of the people, no church except the event itself.

On a collective level it was a kind of self-enquiry, a search for self-knowledge by means of calling the past back into the present, clarifying and integrating memory as an encouragement for entering the unseen future. 'Secular', in a general sense, because any religious words or even deep psychology explicitly stated would have introduced a distorting level of self-consciousness. This is quite typical of the English, of course; formal religion is rarely spoken about in polite society. Perhaps this is because they remember their wars of religion and the very English settlement, Anglicanism, that domesticated and pacified the problem of different gods. But the sacred is present and it can be felt collectively in odd places and at surprising moments. If not actually acknowledged, it is not actively rejected. Where the Spirit is, there is unity. What unifies us while respecting our uniqueness is sacred.

Stories are better than sermons. The two rarely mix well. A good story in a sermon can provide welcome relief from the didactic tone. But it has a design on us and we are suspicious of that. S. T. Coleridge said he hated poetry that 'has a palpable design on us', and, of course, preachers don't tell stories or preach sermons for the sheer joy of it. Stories by nature should be left to stand or fall alone. People are best allowed to draw their own conclusions, which will depend on their level of attention and interest. It was not necessary to praise Henry Cook for his fortitude or heroism. Just remember his way of lifting his pint, and his reputation for cheerfulness.

A gathering of a people who feel connected, like a living community with a shared social and genetic history, creates a special dimension of time: liturgical time, not just the secular time where we charge by the hour. It is like the time busy people make to pray each day. This – let's call it 'sacred' – time leaves the past behind and breaks the negative bonds that keep us trapped there. But simultaneously it brings the past up to date and integrates it. It bans nostalgia as well as the bitterness of history. Through this special portal of time, the *kairos* moment rises through the tick-tock of *chronos*. The storytelling allows the really important people to stand out, people like Henry Cook.

It is hard for religious people not to look at this in relation to their experience of church. For most people this experience has no longer any meaning. But for many it does, and new ways of understanding the liturgical life of a community are emerging as the congregations contract. Someone told me recently about the Easter liturgies that she no longer attends in church. But as we spoke about the different kinds of time, she remembered something she had forgotten. As a very young child she had intensely believed that the events of Good Friday happened again every year. Even then she knew this could not be. The past does not repeat itself. Yet she believed it. For many years she wondered how this could be.

March 2008

18

Trading

It was a glimpse into an abyss. A dense silence hung over the bank's trading room on the thirtieth floor of a Manhattan skyscraper, a building with the bland prosperous looks of those whose great passion is to climb the corporate ladder. Scores of computers were stacked in straight lines like economy class seats for maximum profit and minimal concern for the occupants. Like separate shrines in a busy temple. Each had its devoted attendant. Most of the traders were PhDs or MBAs, in their twenties or thirties, squeezed elbow to elbow. Physical space is not a human issue in this realm of virtual reality. Some looked up at me and the person who brought me to see it. Their brief, barely registered look reminded me of how the tormented souls looked at Dante on his tour of hell and purgatory.

The difference between these two states of the afterlife is that, though the purgatorial fires are as intense as those of hell, they are not eternal. During hours of work, traders are not permitted to use personal email or mobile phones because of the temptation of insider trading. Trust does not run deep. It is a long, intense working day. Lunchtime is a low priority once the markets are open, but some traders had food on their desks, salads for the fit-looking gym members, fast food for those who had given up on their bodies. Their devotion to work reminded me of a late-night visit, after a talk in a church, to a Las Vegas casino. Rows of flashing fruit machines, stretching endlessly like gravestones in a cemetery, were being fed by another kind of gambler, another kind of devotee.

Both temples maintained a kind of perpetual adoration. Maybe the traders, who played big time, have a better chance of winning, but the collateral cost seemed higher.

I don't mean to be personally dismissive of these hard-working people who keep the world of wealth as we know it going, or to begrudge them the rewards. I just couldn't help but wonder if the reward was worth the soul that is lost in this work. I remarked to my Virgil that it was like looking below decks on a Roman galleon and understanding exactly where the momentum of the ship came from and also the condition of the slaves. This system exploits brain rather than brawn, but with equal ruthlessness. Later she told me she had passed on my remark and they smiled and understood.

Trading rooms like this digitalize money around the world, making and breaking fortunes in an empire of high risk and higher abstraction. No dirty fingers of bank clerks counting notes at the counter here. Unlike the Roman galley slaves, however, the traders are reimbursed by bonuses of magnitudes that offer some major consolation for the stress and solitude of the work. On a good day the atmosphere was probably more bullish. The particular mood of depression that hung over the room on my visit was due to a leak about the bank's policy of downsizing.

Eager to offload some of its traders without liability it had just announced provocatively low bonuses. Everybody got the message. The disappointed traders compared their bonus with that of their friends in other institutions. Many had, as the management intended, started looking for a new job. No one knew who was on the severance list or who was staying, or if the elbow next to them would be there next week. When everyone in the crew is jumping ship or wondering if they should, *esprit de corps* is understandably affected. It was not a happy ship that day. But perhaps profit not happiness is the higher priority anyway. The mood was like that of people who do not expect to be happy, at least not at work.

Some of the crew and their officers on the galleon of investment banking know that it does not have to be like this. The inhumanity of impersonally managed institutions like the one I visited is under peer review. After all, it is still purgatory not hell we are dealing with here. There *are* other ways of doing business.

I know a financial top executive who went out on a long personal limb to save some staff who had been unfairly accused of malpractice but were becoming scapegoats in a higher-level political game. Their boss could have let them take the blame and had their careers ruined and their names tarnished. But for him profit happens in a broader context of values. He defended and saved them. Fortunately, his personal risk paid off. His investment of himself in the relationships of his colleagues yielded a higher dividend than money measures: trust, respect, a loyal staff and a happy team buoyed by a sense of security. Using power laterally in this way to affirm personal integrity changes the currency rates on which all trade operates.

As we left the trading room and plummeted down in the high-speed lift I asked my guide if she felt the way of treating people in this unhappy institution was sustainable. She asked if I meant for the people or for the bank. *That* was a worrying question, which might raise the market value of true values.

March 2007

19

William Johnston SJ

Honesty is a rare thing; perhaps because, as Mark Twain said, truth is so precious it should be used sparingly. Sometimes it is hidden behind platitudes and stereotypes that, once they are exposed, unveil the mystery of truth. Sometimes you feel people really are trying to tell the truth as they have experienced it.

I once asked an Irish cousin, whom I felt was on my Anglo-Saxon wavelength, why the Irish can never answer a question directly. He looked away thoughtfully and replied, 'And why would you be asking that, I wonder?' As a stereotype, the evasive Irishman is as unproveable as another one about Jesuits, that no one, not even God, is ever sure what they are really thinking. This one is disproved by an autobiography of an Irish Jesuit, William Johnston's *Mystical Journey*, which, to my delight, he recently sent me. It is a powerful work; not a literary masterpiece perhaps, but it possesses rare clarity, self-knowledge and maybe genuine humility. Here is a priest, a great Jesuit, whose thinking about his own life you can trust and feel better for knowing. He attempts the hardest of all tasks, of telling the truth about himself.

His other books have titles like *Silent Music*, *The Inner Eye of Love*, *Mystical Theology*. Now, in his eighties, comes his honest, plainly told story of a life spent seeking truth. He tells it in short conversational sentences with an apparent ease of self-disclosure. He is open about his struggles with his vow of chastity and movingly describes how they were eventually resolved by discovering the sacred meaning of friendship. More surprising, perhaps, is to learn for how long he struggled with his depth of anger against the British.

Born and reared in Belfast in the 1920s and raised by a fiercely republican mother, he unsurprisingly absorbed the sectarian image of the Protestant oppressor. When I first met him 20 years ago we realized that he had left for Japan the year I was born and has spent more than 50 years there. When he arrived in Tokyo he carried the mentality of his time. Standing in a bus one day he saw that he was the only white person there and the thought came to him that he was the only one on the bus who, at that moment, would be saved. He later came a long way in his understanding of mission and respect for Japanese culture.

At that meeting I asked him if after so many years there he felt he was 'Japanese'. He thought a while and said, in an Irish way but also telling the truth, 'The longer I live there the more I understand what the Japanese really think of foreigners.' In that conversation I also received the first vivid glimpse, in his raised voice and intense gaze, into his still passionate anger at the injustice of the society he grew up in. It was many years before he felt freed from the effects of that anger on his inner peace. During this period he became a pioneer in inter-religious dialogue, influenced by meeting with Pedro Aruppe, the revered superior general of the Jesuits, Thomas Merton and the Japanese novelist Shusaku Endo, and Takashi Nagai, the mystic of Nagasaki. These encounters, his research and his own meditation meant that his knowledge of the mystical wisdom of the East helped him to introduce his Christian students and readers to their own contemplative traditions. He was always clear of the need to belong to your own tradition in order to make dialogue work.

As he tells it, his life is a story of liberation from social and family conditioning, as well as the never-finished struggle fully to embrace one's vocation. He tells it with a disarming humility and transparency. When I said it was not a literary masterpiece I meant not to disparage but to praise it. There is little artifice in it but much *alatheia* – unveiling of the truth.

It reminded me of a talk given by the Dalai Lama in the National Cathedral in Washington DC. I had urged some of my George-town students to go. They stood in line for a long time to get in the back of the church. After many formal introductions, prayers, noble words and compliments, the Dalai Lama walked up into the pulpit and spoke simply for about 15 minutes. His message was very simple and endearing. I can't remember his exact theme, maybe it was about reality and the problem of desire. But everyone was taken by surprise when, at one point, he gave a hearty, self-disparaging laugh and pointed to his lower regions, illustrating his ideas of illusion by referring to the sexual dreams that visit even the best Buddhist monks at times. As I talked with the students later I wondered whether they felt the long wait and the short talk had been worth the effort. They unreservedly did. They felt awakened and stimulated by his words – not by their complexity and formal-ity but by his naturalness. His humour and lack of self-importance made them trust him. They felt he was telling them the truth as he saw it and that afterwards they knew what he was thinking. Rare among religious figures today, especially in relation to the young, he had the kind of authority that is given rather than demanded.

William Johnston in his way tells the truth as his life has taught him about it. In the end it must be this love of truth that keeps life truly alive. When I finished the book I called Bill to thank him for its courage and honesty. We talked about his future travels and I asked if he was coming to North America. He said in an excited voice – 'no – China. That's the future!' Writing a good auto-biography no doubt means you can leave the past behind and look to the future.

October 2007

20

Lambs and Terrorists

It isn't quite a farm in the ordinary sense, but nor would you mistake it for the home of a gentleman farmer or a tourist dude ranch. Two parked trailers, tumble-down shed, roaming hens, roosters, goats, cats and dogs, the farmyard methodically littered with pipes, crates, tools, sacks of things and piles of the rushes she uses for her weaving – a place of daily industry.

It is both home and workplace for a woman who is a gifted basket weaver and sculptor and her partner. Eccentric, even marginal, people if you met them in a city or suburb, but exhibiting a rare sanity here in a small island community as people who know how they want to live and are content. A desert father once remarked, 'The time is coming when people will go mad and then they will point to a sane person and say *he* is mad because he is not like us.' It renews your joy and hope to meet sane people but today you have to be prepared for the fact they may not look at all sane. The weaver has an intense look, holds eye contact for more than two seconds (enough to make most people today appear insane) and brims over with energy and humour. She has the edgy humility of a working artist and an earthy body language, and she seems genuinely interested in you as part of the world she also inhabits.

I walked into the chaotic yard and was attacked by a magpie that the weaver had saved and that has now become a very eccentric bird. It will even play a fly-and-fetch game like a dog with wings. As the weaver's partner came to greet me I noticed a lamb emerge from the shed following him. I asked if they were now keeping sheep as well. The lamb seemed as odd as the magpie as it kept approaching, held in the man's orbit. Sheep don't usually bond with people as closely as some parables suggest. Then I noticed it was also walking somewhat oddly, unsteady on its four wobbly legs as if someone had slipped something into its grain that morning. It stopped beside us, like a child clinging to its parent or a dog seeking company, and gave off the emotional bonding that makes us feel that dogs love us. It looked at me looking at it, with the same directness as its protectors, and seemed to say, 'I am not an ordinary lamb. I want to be your friend too.'

As I couldn't follow this up directly with the lamb I asked its human spokesman who said that, yes, it *was* an odd little creature. The maternal weaver had cared for it round the clock when, very soon after its birth, it seemed by the ordinary course of nature set to die. It was diagnosed with meningitis, inflammation of the brain and spinal cord. Later I looked it up and found that this was indeed an illness of sheep. My book on sheep disease says, 'The affected lamb can't stand and its rear quarter is weak. The brain is infected. Antibiotics may help but the prognosis is guarded.'

For the time being this particular lamb, mentally and physically damaged, had beaten the statistics and was moreover assured of a caring environment for the rest of its days. However nonproductive and expendable in the war of evolution, conducted endlessly on the battlefield of Nature, it would always be safe here. There was something incurably sane and noble about this human care for a useless, damaged member of another species.

The breaking news that evening was about some bombs disguised as printer cartridges discovered in the freight of a number of planes. Damaged people who didn't care for their own species very well had managed to carry some on to passenger flights, intending the slaughter of hundreds of individuals that the perpetrators of the crime had no interest in personally. The only importance to the bombers of the people they had selected as their victims was to be sacrificial victims, like the lambs once slaughtered in the Temple of Jerusalem. Perhaps what shocks and terrifies us most about terrorism is its coldness, its dehumanized impersonality.

Part of the terror that hits the survivors and the rest of the world is that it proves how far the human can regress from itself, not merely into the pre-human but into a total degeneration of its own nature. Nothing else in the natural world, however deformed or inadequate for survival, is capable of this perversion of its own nature. However much we condemn it, we are implicated and accused by the simple fact of its occurrence. If 'they' can do this, might not I be capable of something equally inhuman? This is part of the fascination of evil that keeps us studying the Holocaust. I was part of a dialogue once between a Christian Polish advocate of Jewish–Christian relations and some old women who had survived the camps. The Christian was full of intense collective guilt, but the women wanted to use the perspective that 70 years had given them, including the ability to forget. One woman leant over to the other and said, 'He is taking this so personally.' The other nodded and turned to him kindly and said, 'We know that if you'd been there you wouldn't have done these things to us.' He looked at her with something between pathos and absurdity and said, 'That's the thing. I don't know that.'

Natural human empathy is inverted. Just as we feel proud when we hear of human courage and altruism, so we feel humiliated and degraded by human inhumanity.

Security experts say that an expert bomb-maker is like a painter. He has a personal style that makes him stand out. How like art, in some Halloween inversion of holiness, the skills of destructions are. We speak of the 'art of war' and divert the creative imagination from works that bless to those that maim with maximum efficiency. My weaver friend and her brain-damaged lamb seem so eccentric, unimportant and marginal beside this scale of violence. The stoney-heartedness of those inflamed with hatred seem undefeatable beside the silly, sublime, tender care a human can give an ovine invalid. What can cure the inflamed mind of a terror merchant and turn his heart of stone to flesh except infinitely more of the weaver's wasted love.

November 2010

21

The Stingray and the Djinns

My godson, 4-year-old Colum, made me a Christmas present of a drawing and told me that it was about Jesus. What is that? Jesus in the manger. And that? Joseph. And that (a long squiggly line)? A stingray. I looked unsurprised. So as not so disturb the universe I had entered, I didn't ask why it was there. Indeed, why not? What is so special about lambs and oxen? Why shouldn't there have been a stingray in Bethlehem? But I thought I could ask where Mary was. You can't see her, she's behind the stingray. I nodded.

The *Dhammapada* says that the world is what we make it, the total construction of our thoughts. Jesus points to this when he says that where your heart is there your treasure will be. How we act is shaped by what we see. If we are blinded by desire or fear, that colours or obscures everything else. Our way of perception *shapes* our experience of reality. This stays the case until something outside our frame of reference leaps down from a throne of silence and rearranges our world so that its total otherness becomes intimate with us. This is the great epiphany of Christian faith. Colum introduced the stingray, as alien as God to the material world, into a familiar and predictable picture of reality.

Of course, Colum's invincibility, like the daring of youth, is the powerful charm of innocence and many allowances can be made because of that. But his perception, in its own moment, is *certain*. It so stuns the adult mind because of the quite different way he has of believing what is a certainty. Our own self-doubts and contradictions are exposed, we question what we thought we had understood and see how little we know for certain.

Sharing his world in this way at that moment reminded me of another child's universe whose outer edge I once brushed. Wearing my white habit, I went to meditate with a class of preschoolers in the Townsville diocese, where meditation has become part of religious education in all Catholic schools. I noticed a little girl watching me with fascination as the other children ran around to get the meditation circle ready. When I asked her for her name she just continued to stare at me. After a few more attempts at conversation I wondered if she couldn't speak. Then she approached me cautiously and looked at me curiously and asked, 'Are you an angel?'

It was the disempowering question of a very young mind and it silenced my mind. It had no irony or duplicity. If her teacher had said it I would have felt some hostility or mockery. Like the stingray by the manger, it simply had to be acknowledged and accepted. Prudence is needed in responding to this kind of view of the world. Roughly contradicting or trivializing such a childlike perception of reality would deserve a millstone around one's neck. A child's view of the world has its own self-affirming certainty and a child's creativity can provide explanations for many of the questions that challenge it. Mary can't be seen because she's behind the stingray. Eventually, though, and one hopes by gentle stages, other horizons of perception emerge and the child will yield its self-sufficiency and recognize an objective order of reality – maybe not the only order, but real enough to be taken seriously.

Pressed upon by bigger galaxies in the same cosmos that we inhabit, we open up to them and expand. Mythical certainties yield somewhat and accommodate to the rational. Later, the self-sufficiency of reason is in its turn challenged by a larger perception and surrenders itself in order to enter the realm of perception of the non-dual, the vision of unity that comes when the eye of the heart is opened.

We all live together, and our different universes jostle against each other. This cohabiting of different visions of the world may be seen in any Shakespeare play; and the wonder of life demands a catholicity always bigger than our private world. If we lack this tolerance we will no longer be surprised by reality and we will perish from boredom. Or we will run from boredom by destroying or colonizing what is different from us.

Part of the ritual of gift-giving is to conceal the gift so as to accentuate the delight of eventually seeing it. The Fathers of the Church say that the incarnation both reveals and hides divinity. The story that follows the nativity is a tragical farce of misrecognition and misunderstanding. 'He comes to us hidden and salvation consists in our recognizing him,' Simone Weil tells us. What is this re-cognition, this expansion of the horizon of our perceptions, except entering the 'new creation' where we finally get it right, where certainty and truth are united and perception and reality are one?

The perceptions that create the world of children are easy to accept because they are protected from us by their innocence; and we are protected from them because we know they will change. With older people the way we see the world can be more challenging.

I met once with an old Iranian living in Mumbai, quite a worldly and sharp, hoary individual. In the same way that doctors get unsolicited case histories from fellow dinner guests who in the course of conversation have discovered their profession, religious people are often treated to strangers' unsolicited explanations about how the world is made and what God really wants of us. Our conversation in the Iranian's tenement building in Mumbai was a little one-sided as he was not as interested in my world as he evidently thought I should be in his. But I was permitted a visit to the very different reality that he inhabited.

Jalal told me about *djinns*, creatures made of fire that cohabit our world but are invisible. They are often mischievous, but sometimes those who have prayed and fasted enough can see them. He looked round the room. Yes, they were there as we spoke. In response to my questions, eager for more information of his world, he responded in a way similar to Colum's account of why Mary couldn't be seen. Jalal waved his hand sagely and confessed that he only knew a very little about *djinns*. But there were many wiser Zoroastrians than him I could consult.

This doesn't mean to imply that Jalal was childish. Rather more disturbingly, it suggests that we are all strongly inclined to think that our belief system is right or righter than others. And so to avoid the errors of pride, whatever our explanation for things and the way we see the world may be, our concepts and theories should always be exposed to fundamental questions

Who would disagree that there is more in our world-view or belief system than anyone can fully understand? Science admits that as little as 4 per cent of the matter in the cosmos is made of known material. A shared humility about what we admit we don't know may unite us even more than most of what we feel certain about. As the *Cloud of Unknowing* said, 'We can never know God by thought but only by love.'

So, after meeting the *djinns*, I decided that at the next opportunity I would ask Colum an obvious question I had neglected to ask earlier, about how the stingray got to Bethlehem.

January 2007

22

Church of the Trinity
and the Dropouts

Salvador is a city in the tropical north-east of Brazil. The first
Benedictine monastery outside Europe was founded here. San
Sebastiano still has the long, wide corridors that suit the climate
and the slow-motion style of life. The original hard-wood floors
shine with the soft friction of many generations of monks, and
the large, whitewashed cells have changed little since the colonial
period. Meals, as in most monasteries, are choreographed rituals
of efficient eating and social engineering, preserving charity and
good order at the same time because both are necessary. The meals,
like everything in the life, are framed in the language of prayer. As
individuals the monks are friendly but reserved.

In the lower and poorer part of town is the dilapidated Church
of the Trinity and another type of community. Its once prosperous congregation migrated to more affluent neighbourhoods and
left the church empty for many years. Today it is home to the
Communidade da Trinidade. Lunch here is very, but not wholly,
different to meals in the tranquil monastery.

The community is made up of street people. The food is cooked
on a wooden stove in the open air. The young woman responsible
for cooking that noon hour was anxious because the meal was a
little late. It was rice and beans (again) but the watermelon looked
(and was) irresistible. The food was placed on a long serving table.
Rough wooden benches lined the peeling walls for the community

and their guests. Brother Henrique, the community's leader, read slowly from the gospel and then prayed and welcomed us. Beside me was Maria, a large, deranged but exuberant personality. She had survived, lived a life of abuse on the streets and for many years had been made drunk and sexually exploited by men. Her toothless smile belied years of degradation, but she was gradually being redeemed by love and the sense of acceptance she found in this community. The meal did not have the choreographic elegance of the monastery but it too was a sacrament, informal, relaxed and in its way orderly and dignified by the respect it expressed for all the types it had gathered. Henrique's authority was observant, like an abbot's, but gentle, and it conveyed peace.

All the members of the community are street people. Most are struggling with drugs or alcohol or coming out of years of prostitution. Their histories were written in their eyes and in the cautious way they had learned to rest in the friendship of the older members. They were learning the meaning of one of Benedict's great insights, expressed as one of the vows, stability. This made the other quality of Benedict's vision of life, the practice of hospitality, more real. Each night they, and many others who turn up for shelter and food, sleep on cardboard mats on the floor of the church.

I first met Henrique, short, wiry and ascetic, five years before when he attended a meditation retreat, recently I met him again on another retreat. For many years he had obeyed the call to follow Jesus as he travelled as a homeless pilgrim around Brazil. Like the Russian Pilgrim, he prayed continuously as he walked and when he was moved on by the police. When he came to Salvador he began to sleep on the floor of this abandoned church that sits on a hill in a *favella* and overlooks the rough and dangerous district of the old port. Centuries ago a French community working for the liberation of slaves had started the church. When others began to take shelter there with him, Henrique asked the diocese for the church. This was granted and the roof was repaired. But apart from being dry it is rough, part dormitory, part drop-in centre for drop-outs, part place of worship.

Morning and evening prayer incorporate a period of silent meditation which the street people love. Outside, a few metres higher than the church building, there is a small lush garden and a couple of single rooms, which Henrique proudly shows me as their hermitage, They are used by the members of the community and sometimes by priests of the diocese who come to refresh their demanding ministries with the poor.

When I asked Henrique what happened if members of the community went back on to drugs or drink, I understood how remarkable this tropical epiphany of the Kingdom – and of gospel life – really is. Like any abbot, when asked what his monks do or how many there are in community, he said, 'It all depends.' Each person is a unique case. The good of the individual and of the whole have to be balanced. Living with a person taking drugs makes life even harder for those trying to quit. But community helps the addict to quit again. The point is that the community is not a social project, measuring success by the rehabilitation of its clients, but a community. At the heart of every community, as of every family, is an unconditional acceptance, forgiveness before the fall.

It would be easy to mistake this place for a social centre or a refuge for the homeless, but it is even more. It is in fact a serious contemplative community that, like any other, has its problems and odd personalities. Prayer is at the heart of their life. It regulates the rhythms of the day, just as in a monastery. At the heart of the prayer is a spirit of active love. When people leave, Henrique said, they are bidden farewell as gently, as non-possessively as they were once welcomed. No success, so no failure. What matters, he said, smiling with his shining eyes, is that they can remember, maybe at some desperate moment of loneliness on the streets again, that they once had their dignity recognized and were truly loved.

December 2008

23

Bhikkuni

Even though it sits beside a busy highway, an hour's torturous drive from the city, after the polluted chaos of Bangkok, Bhikkuni Dhammananda's centre is a fresh, green haven. Instead of diesel fumes you can again smell earth and the scent of flowers. The vegetation in the garden is lush and rampant. Dhammananda is one of only eight fully ordained Buddhist women monastics in Thailand. She is a strong personality, head shaved, robed like a monk, every inch an abbess. She greets us warmly, but like all Theravada monks she eats once a day, at noon. As in any monastery, feeding and praying times are equally sacrosanct. So she excuses herself and sends us off to explore while she has lunch with her community.

In Thailand, with a population of 62 million, there are 300,000 monks (*bhikkus*). Numbers are decreasing as westernized stress erodes the leisure necessary for monasticism. In a monastery, leisure as well as discipline is essential for the regulation of the contemplative practice and for maintaining mental calm. By the standards of modern economics this leisure is laziness. Leisure is justified only when it refreshes the worker for more production. Traditional monastic – and Buddhist – values in Thailand have been strongly affected by its economic development. Fewer boys and men with career prospects feel they have time to be monks. Some people think that this reduction in numbers is beneficial because temporary monastic ordination is generally little more than a socialized ritual. All males are expected to become a monk once in their life, even for a month, in order to gain and transfer merit to their parents. The rare and anxiously considered idea of monastic vocation we are familiar with in the West does not fit this pattern. Many poor boys are still given to a Buddhist monastery, as were oblates in St Benedict's time, to relieve financial pressure on the family and to gain a basic education.

Buddhism is the state religion of the Kingdom of Thailand, and the monastic sangha is legislated into the national constitution. By a reactive law of 1928, prompted by a challenge to what Dhammananda calls the structural violence against women, it became illegal to ordain women as *bhikunnis*. Those who wanted to live a religious life have had to do so as a *maechee*. These are white- (not saffron-) robed nuns who are widely associated with performing the domestic functions that keep the temples and monks' residences comfortable and clean. A few of these half-nuns have earned a reputation as spiritual teachers but they remain of inferior status and are denied access to the higher education restricted to males.

When Bhikunni Dhammananda returns to us we sit at the stone table overlooking the garden while she gives us a vigorous account of the history of the entrenched prejudice she is contesting. Like the few other fully ordained Thai women, she went to Sri Lanka, leaving a university career, a marriage and family of her own, to express the full form of her monastic calling. I tell her she reminds me a little of Sr Joan Chittister, the radical American Benedictine nun who has confronted similar issues in the Catholic Church. I am not so surprised when Dhammananda says she knows Sr Joan and has collaborated with her on various projects. I ask her what she thinks lies behind the patriarchal obstructionism and exclusion of women. In response she asks me if she can speak directly. I say I expect she will and she does: 'Power and money,' she says.

No doubt these are big considerations. The shadow side of many religions is the way they get caught up in the very wealth and status that they teach others to transcend. But remembering the story of the Buddha's first response to women's ordination, I felt the reasons for the subordination of women in religion goes deeper than that.

After his enlightenment at the age of 35 the Buddha tied the spread of his teaching to the monastic order he founded. When the Buddha's father died, his stepmother, Queen Mahapajapati, asked the Buddha for permission to follow him in the monastic state. He replied, 'Please do not ask so.' Undeterred, she later arrived before him with a train of 500 women with shaved heads and yellow robes. The Buddha gave the same response. Ananda, his beloved disciple, asked if it was because women could not achieve enlightenment, but the Buddha affirmed that women and men have equal spiritual potential – a historic statement in the history of religion. So, Ananda asked, why can't they be monks? The Buddha relented and *bhikunnis* became accepted. The problem returned soon after his death, however, and, as Bhikunni Dhammananda's story testifies, the position of women in most Buddhist cultures rapidly degenerated.

The story of the Buddha and the Queen oddly echoes one about St Benedict and his sister, the nun St Scholastica. He used to come down from Monte Casino to visit her. On one occasion, as their conversation was so enjoyable, she pressed him to stay longer. Obedient to his own rule not to stay outside the monastery, he refused. She then prayed for a change in the weather and a huge storm broke and forced him to stay there overnight. He berated her. But she had got her way.

Perhaps the reason that men in general, not only monks, need to dominate women is not just wealth and power but also fear. They fear that otherwise they will become subordinated to them. The mother–son relationship is not an equal one and for most monks (like the Buddha) it may be the strongest relationship they ever have with a woman. Bhikunni Dhammananda is not competing with the monks. She bides her time, and time is on her side, and she isn't trying to frighten them unnecessarily. But modernity has hit Thai Buddhism as it has struck all religions.

April 2008

24

Desley and Death

As she lay in bed, her morphine drip keeping her pain-free and clear-minded, Desley was anxious about her garden. Over the last months of her three-year illness it had been neglected. She wanted it tidied up before she died. Her four beautiful daughters, as strong-willed as their mother but completely under her thumb, had cared for her lovingly at every stage of her physical decline. They had also tried to keep up with – and understand – her spiritual ascent. They jumped at her commands as if they were 20 years younger.

One of the girls came in to tell Desley that the gardener had finished and needed to be paid. How much and where was the money? Desley answered as decisively as she had run the house for years as a single parent. The only man in the room admired how a woman runs the complex affairs of a home and keeps all the strands of relationship in her hands.

As she now found it hard to move in bed I suggested taking the mirror off the wall and positioning it on a table near the window, angled so she could see what was going on outside. We worked at this for a while, though I thought it was what was going on inside that really attracted her attention and she spoke of her changing inner landscape. Then we were aware that the gardener had entered the room. With the physical presence of someone who works outdoors, he just wanted to see Desley. He described what he had done in the garden, but the fact that she wouldn't be here to see the end of the summer hung unspoken in the air. There would be more work in the next season and he spoke matter of factly about that. Then with a casual farewell he took his leave.

Alone, Desley and I spoke about her latest project for the community. She was born in Mount Isa, a remote mining town in Northern Queensland, became a musician and came to England. When she first heard about meditation she knew she had found the missing piece in her already full life. She grew into the community more as her meditation deepened and became an integral part of daily life. Her girls accepted the time this took but she never tried to force it on to them. As the UK national co-ordinator, she founded the Christian Meditation retreat centre in London. She loved this work. And she loved nothing better than getting the house ready. One day, as she was pulling a chest of drawers around a room, her back twinged painfully and did not stop hurting as she accompanied me on a short tour of Wales. It was the first sign of the melanoma.

In this last phase of her life she was still coming up with new ideas and plans for the community. She began to tell me about what would be her last project. Every few minutes she would take a sip of water to refresh her mouth. She had not swallowed anything solid for three weeks. Yet with great enthusiasm she showed me a design for an interfaith medallion she wanted to have made. The idea came to my mind a week later while I was talking to a learned Jesuit about his conviction that any truth – wherever it is found – must be not only reverenced but actively promoted in that form. Desley's design of the interlinking symbols of many traditions expressed the same idea. It also characterized her own passion for truth. Because she found it explicitly in Christ did not mean she did not also recognize it elsewhere, everywhere. Her last project summed up her life's journey into God.

She was content. She felt at peace and in a state of continuous joy. But she could not understand why she was still here. She was a Martha who was on good terms with Mary. What good was she serving anyone any more? Why hadn't he come and taken her home? 'He pokes his head round the door every so often,' she said. 'But when I turn he's gone again. But I'm watching for him and next time I'll catch him and won't let him go.'

Was she curious about what would come next? St Bernard said curiosity about things that do not directly concern our salvation should be rejected, but that there is such a thing as holy curiosity. No, she answered with certainty, she was not curious about the next world. She thought and added, 'I think I know what it's like.' I waited. It would be like just what she was living now, except more. Profound peace, unbelievable spiritual energy, joyousness and love. These are only marks on the page, only words. Spoken by her then it was one of those rare moments in conversation that words meant exactly and everything they were supposed to mean.

Perhaps this is why Jesus didn't feed our curiosity about what happens in the next phase of life? Our questions miss the answer, which is already contained in the time and place in which we are asking them. I understood better how the resurrection is less about the 'next life' and more about living this one in a new way. Because there is only one life. Desley at that instant was one of those who teach this and serve its truth just by being who they are here and now. The metaphysics of death dissolved and there was just life. Sitting with her, as she paid the gardener, bossed her daughters and looked into the window of her soul, showed what the present moment means.

Her years of meditation and unstinting care for her family were coming together. She could let go of them but would never give up. Self-giving had long combined with her strong Aussie personality and her homemaker's practicality. It was now as full as the house she lived in. It was being tidied up like the garden. She was becoming an open window, a person without clinging. When the angle was right you could see a long way into the garden and what the gardener had been doing there for many seasons.

October 2008

25

Manaus

Eduardo Goncalves Ribeiro had a tropical personality. He was born in Amazonia in 1890. His mother was a slave but he grew to be twice governor of the new Brazilian State of Amazonas. Ribeiro more than anyone was responsible for its constitution, which he conceived on democratic, positivist principles that, controversially, confronted the Church's interference in secular affairs. He visited Europe and dreamed the dream of turning his capital of Manaus into the 'Paris of the Tropics'. Never married, his work was his life and he rode the high wave of the late nineteenth-century Brazilian rubber boom. Manaus today is much dilapidated, but the great buildings, especially the famous opera house, witness to the imprint of his fertile personality on the city. The opera house is now renovated for the more imaginative tourists who venture this far inland away from the familiar. Its chandeliers are of Murano glass, its marble stairs from Cararra, its steel walls from Glasgow, the interior furnishing from France and its roof tiles from Alsace.

Ribeiro ruled over a brief human world both mirroring and competing with the natural world within which it defiantly carved itself a space: the impenetrable vegetation of the jungle and the flamboyant creatures of the animal kingdom teeming around it on all sides. The surreal costumes of Carnevale reflect the divine imagination playfully at work in the crests of birds and the heart-opening beauty of the inside of butterfly wings that seem like silent messages of the cosmic design. Within the rampant jungle, Ribeiro cleared a civilization of grand public buildings, parks and gardens, racecourses and bullrings and fine restaurants. It wanted to imitate the European world but must, as it still does, have always seemed closer to the jungle whose sovereignty it challenged but on which it also depended. The euphoria of the rubber boom, like that of the City of London in the 1990s, often went insane with affluence. Rubber barons, not unlike the robber bankers, lit their cigars with hundred-dollar bills, watered their horses on champagne and sent their laundry to Paris. Their wives sweltered in fur coats in the opera house.

All this came from a white sticky liquid that oozes easily from a cut in the bark of a tree in the jungle. From time unremembered, the indigenous people had used its elastic properties, but Charles Goodyear refined the production process and gave the world the rubber tyres that it still runs on today. True to their noble history of patriotic piracy, it was the English who punctured the Manaus dream. In 1867 Henry Wickham, later knighted for his criminal mission, on instructions from the botanical director of Kew Gardens in London, smuggled out of the country seeds of the all-important *Hervea Brasiliensis* rubber tree. By 1920, 90 per cent of the world's rubber came from British plantations in Asia.

Like economists coping in today's financial crisis, Manaus made desperate efforts to prevent what was the inevitable collapse of Amazonia's brief and eccentric glory. With his astute political intelligence, Ribeiro must have seen the end coming. One day in 1900, at the age of 38, he was found hanged in his study, sitting in his rocking chair. They said that the voices he had always heard screaming in his head must have become unbearable. One cannot even hover on the margins of his extravagant yet strangely lonely and unfulfilled life without the kind of wonder and sheer gratitude for life that you feel riding up the mighty Amazon by canoe or cutting your way a few metres into the dense jungle. As you fall asleep in a hammock in a hard-won clearing you know that almost perceptibly the jungle is moving in to replace what you have removed.

You wonder, drowsing in the milky moonlight bathing the world around you, whether the jungle will not have imprisoned you by morning. As Ribeiro discovered, whether in the jungle where he was born or in the urban clearing he made, once you let life loose it can be lived but not controlled.

Ribeiro made many mistakes, as there must be many seeds that fall and disintegrate unfertilized in the self-reproducing imagination of the jungle. Not least of Ribeiro's was the hollow hubris of his plan, which, like that of all imperious attempts to dominate the world, became intoxicated on the fantasy of an eternal success. Nothing lasts for ever and most things don't last long. But, unlike the animals or the canopy of tress extending thousands of miles in all directions, or the vegetation in its hungry cycle, human beings deny death. We convince ourselves that what we create may be, may just be, immortal. The jungle on a daily basis and the longer sweep of human history repeat the only immortal wisdom: that life is cyclical and that its cycles depend on nadirs, the bottom-points of death, and the climaxes of the peaks of rebirth.

Despite its fall, Manaus is still there, welcoming people to the Amazon. What consoles us for the pain of human stupidity that we learn from its history is just what the ecology of the jungle teaches by its symphony of life and death, decay and regeneration. In the forest you tread on the abundant evidence that the worst failures serve as sediment for new waves of life that take us endlessly by surprise and over which we have little control. This moment of joyful powerlessness in every life cycle is the spring from which the fountain of creation flows. It is like the point at land's end where a river becomes a waterfall as it drops hundreds of metres into the new channel in which it will next flow. Musically, to hear this, listen to Beethoven's last piano sonata.

Maybe this irrepressible hope in the cycle of life was one of those intolerable voices that competed for Ribeira's attention at the end. Maybe he had never lost the contact with the jungle he was born in. Or perhaps, like most of us today with our artificial environments and television nature programmes, he had moved too far from the jungle to be able to hear the wisdom it teaches.

September 2012

26

Haiti

We arrived during the children's lunchtime. Mother Teresa once visited the orphanage in Port au Prince, Haiti, and, rarely for her, had been taken sick during her stay. One Dutch Missionary of Charity has the look of someone in love. She cares for the babies as attentively as if she began as a novice a month ago. She has been here for 30 years. She recalls Mother's visit with affection. But speaks with a deep kind of love not about her foundress but the children who, since that visit, have been arriving into their care in increasing numbers. Some are left by desperate mothers on the doorstep; others are brought temporarily to recover from malnutrition.

This is the nation's capital. Capital of the poorest and most ignored country in the western hemisphere. In 1803 Haitians became the first slaves in history successfully to revolt against their masters, and they bought their freedom from France in cash. In recent history a succession of brutal dictators destroyed their freedom and hope. Yet even in Creole, the formal courtesies of their language and perhaps pure faith itself lift this battered and abused people above their miseries.

The babies lie in cots with high railings. There are as many as can fit into the rooms and still leave space for the sisters to pass by and give the children whatever fleeting individual attention they can. The children are all lovingly cared for but of course they cannot belong to those who care for them as a child needs to belong. It is a home for the homeless. The children look up with big appealing eyes from the deep silence of their lonely limbos. How cruelly disassociated from reality was the scholastic idea that God sent unbaptized children to perpetual limbo where they wouldn't even have had Mother Teresa's sisters to look after them. When they cry the children seem desperately trying to connect but bitterly aware that it is already too late for the kind of connection they crave. The wounds they have received will be with them for life.

In a few cots two siblings lie together, their tiny limbs interlocking. Their worlds seem less astronomically distant than the others. On the streets and in the villages, too, but here in the children's home especially, I see the vast gulf between our worlds. As Abraham coldly told the rich man suffering hellfire for failing during his lifetime to care for the beggar Lazarus, 'Between us and you there is a great gulf fixed: so that they which would pass from hence to you cannot; neither can they pass to us, that would come from thence.'

I sit by the cot of a solitary boy about 2 years old. He is sitting cross-legged in the corner of the cot and as far up against the farthest rail as he can get. He looks at me, his big white eyes like lamps in his shiny, black skin. He looks but he cannot trust. I put my hand out to touch him. He pushes it away with all his meagre force. One day his power of rejection will be stronger. Now in his frailty it seems only like a symbolic gesture. His wounded heart is not wholly in it. It is already a reflex he is mastered by. The boy looks at me in pain, defiantly and defensively as I keep trying to bridge that great gulf with a bowl of food. When I put my hand into the cot a few inches in front of him, he looks at it, considers the options and then slaps it. His little hand striking at something so much bigger might seem funny. But this is not a short sulk from a terrible two. It is trauma not tantrum. The traumatic experience – loss, abandonment, not understanding the withdrawal of love – that shook his soul to its core is already inaccessible. What can clothe the suffering undergone before words and concepts are possible? Only love, over a period of time no one here can give, could reach so far back.

Eventually he accepts small pieces of food and looks interested in them, but those small transactions are not yet a basis for emotional negotiation. Love is patient, must persevere, as the sister who has been at it for 30 years has discovered. I have to leave with my fellow meditator pilgrims, slowly forming the conviction that only deep prayer can change all this. Not easy petitionary prayers. But the prayer that painfully changes the one who prays.

It was hard to leave the little boy. Though he was probably relieved I had left and stopped invading his space, it made me feel a failure. It might take years of enduring his rejection before the desperate patterns in which his mind was being set could be dissolved. Like the children being bombed in Gaza or Syria or Somalia, he is one more innocent sacrifice, collateral damage on the ancient altar of violence. Violence comes in many forms, economic, social or military. It is the dogma that still runs the world. Americans, Israeli, Syrian spokesmen talked *sincerely* of their regret at the collateral damage of their wars. They blame the other side. There is always someone to blame to justify the inexcusable. Until prayer or love goes deep enough to change the inner mind there is always an opposing side. There are always victims, and some of them – although only about 50 per cent in Haiti – grow up in a world that has been fractured from the beginning.

January 2009

27

Google

We joked half-seriously that the GPS seemed fixated on Mountain View as every trip we made in the area led us back through that heart, if that is the right word, of Silicon Valley.

People tend to live where they are best suited to survive and where the ambience reflects their personality and expectations. How this generalization applies to a church whose centre is among the nostalgic ruins of a collapsed empire that it once served then succeeded, I'm not sure. But it has a point in relation to a very secular and postmodern company like Google, for whom even the idea of hierarchy seems quaintly redundant. Like a new kind of postman, it sorts and delivers information and services to virtual individuals globally. It seeks ever new ways to do this in the ever more luminous cloud of knowing that is the internet. It dreams and expects to take over, or cover the world as a service to humanity. It says it will 'do no evil'.

What more suitable location for this Google dream and the lifestyle that supports it than California? This far western land has long been the realm of dreams, first as the place where gold flowed freely in the rivers and then as the land of plenty where work and play merge in the pursuit of happiness. The end of the great march from the old world to a new universal freedom and well-being led in the end to the shore of beautiful beaches where you could go no further. The problem starts here, when the dreams create their own feedback and as the settlers really settled down and made a society of phenomenal instability. Having said that, I like California and if

I had to choose I would probably prefer to live in Los Angeles than San Francisco. Strange as they are, or because of their strangeness, I find the Californians very nice people even though most of them of course are not Californian.

When we arrived at Google HQ, the receptionist was away but had left a note asking us to check ourselves in on the computer, help ourselves to drinks and snacks and wait. We looked at the relic of the first huge computer of the company that generated so much heat that its internal fans took up most of its space. Looking at its amazonian trails of wires made one wonder how anyone could ever have fixed it if it overheated or something didn't work. Probably they didn't fix it, we decided. They put it in a museum and invented a better one. This piece of industrial archaeology was only 20 years old. Being ancient at 20, reminded us of the electric speed at which the global virtual knowledge industry has grown. It highlighted this company's brilliant attunement to the raging hunger of our time both for quick answers and a sense of connection.

One in five Americans, it is said, aspire to work at Google. So those who do work here have the feel of people who have won the lottery and can't quite believe it. With their share options, many of the early employees really did win the jackpot. Working conditions are ideal, apparently low-key but very carefully crafted for the brilliant minds they are designed to make even more productive of new and better ideas. As we were shown round it felt more like a spa or recreation centre, free food (no one works more than 100 feet from a (healthy) snack counter), six different cuisines for the predominantly Asian workforce, massage rooms, quick-nap pods, exercise rooms, pool and just places to chill out. Executive perks for everyone.

People seem almost reluctant to admit that they actually work here. They laugh off the idea that there must be some control mechanism behind all this successful happiness. Nowhere more than here you see how Americans have made the old world suspicious or resentful of their innocent pursuit of pleasure. Why can't we make work more like fun? Maybe happy, well-paid work for a successful cutting-edge corporation might even be a substitute for the great metaphysical questions that unnecessarily tormented the old culture for so long. Why must the pursuit of meaning and truth be so painful and create such a trail of loss and failure? Old-world religion created a dystopia of tragic proportion. Why not try for a utopia in the dawning of a new age of instant communication and wish-fulfilment?

Sometimes you see this dilemma in the way an adult listens to a child or adolescent who is evidently talking idealistic nonsense. While knowing that what they are saying is never going to work, the older person cannot but feel admiration and even envy. They listen without wanting to puncture the dream, aware that the only way it could work is if you continue to believe in it that intensely. And who knows? Who are we, the disillusioned, to judge? Yet utopias underpin our most disastrous social experiments.

California is the perennial symbol of this lucid dreaming. It has its armies of homeless, the old waiters whose Hollywood aspirations perished, ugly landfill areas of waste, ghettoes of failure, a vast pornography industry and other dark eruptions of the human shadow. But they are not recognized as real. It is the dream that is real. The rest is zoned away, sometimes out of sight and often out of mind. Ideals and plans become more important than facts and consequences. Google says it will do no evil but it won't give information to the government about its information-gathering tactics.

Google HQ is a centre of global power but not like the Vatican, certainly not like Lambeth Palace and, who knows, maybe less influential than the White House in how we live day by day. But it thinks and acts globally, is prepared to make mistakes in the process of improvement. And it undeniably has ideals. Like anything focused on success, it has had to compromise on its original pure motives and its ideals are somewhat tarnished. But it doesn't dwell on its sin. California doesn't do guilt. It is confidently secular, not anti-religious at all, but free and flexible about deciding subjectively what spiritualities 'work' and what don't. This may, it is true, lead to the arrested spiritual development of many New Age phenomena, a kind of spiritual narcissism. But it's better than the arrested development of the fundamentalist zealot or the sclerotic mind that can operate in religious institutions and that seeks world domination in a different way from Google.

Then there's meditation. A modern, successful corporation like Google sees meditation as a life-skill, an invaluable tool for clear thinking, calm minds and healthy bodies. It makes the stuffier corridors of the corporate world look old-fashionedly uptight. Of course, California thinks it discovered meditation and is now in the process of improving it. Ancient traditions might feel disturbed by this. Or, they might feel surprised by learning from the fresh excitement of people who are in pursuit of all the answers but who haven't yet made the big mistakes that others feel they have to deny.

There are signs of the bubble bursting. I had a conversation with an individual that I first thought was ironical but soon realized was very serious. It was about developing a technology to speed up and control the enlightenment process. If it worked, he said with a triumphant smile, you could become like the Dalai Lama in six weeks. And of course it could be done online.

February 2011

28

Recognizing

I needed some time to prepare quietly before my talk and was trying to find a corner where I could disappear. It's never easy having to cut people short – especially someone you know and haven't seen for a while – and I was finding it difficult to get away. I saw a pass and headed for it. Then I became conscious of someone standing to one side of me, as if allowing me to pass if I wished, but looking at me intently. I glanced at him, intending to be polite but non-engaging. He seemed willing to let me through, but something about his presence held me and I made the crucial pause that gets you delayed by a new conversation. Then he said, 'Hello, Laurence.'

It was a German accent and we were in Paris. I was confused. It was a familiar voice but my memory scouts had to go seeking deep in the vaults to find the right associations. In a moment, when I looked at him with attention, an old friend instantly took the place of the stranger I had failed to recognize. Fifteen intervening years were etched on his face. Older, but I could see also a calmer, deeper yet still intense soul. I didn't need to ask if he was still an artist who sacrificed a lot for his work. He was the artist forever looking at the world with the creative mix of curiosity, pain and hope. From beyond the horizon of memory sailed a rediscovery, something forgotten and restored, another loss completing the cycle of its meaning in a new finding.

A bridge appeared over the canyon of time past and touched time present. It was a happy moment as there is happiness in connection itself. We had not fought, just over the years simply drifted into different slipstreams. But all separation has a slight flavour of guilt – maybe it goes back to the primal separations of birth and death, the feeling we are abandoning a truth. When we meet people again there can be an instant cosmic sense that reunion gives – something that went foolishly, bizarrely wrong, though we didn't realize it at the time, has now been put right again.

Religion itself means to 're-link'. The word 'recognition' has something similar buried in its history. It is not merely the identification of a person that happens in such moments but a kind of resuming of possession of an old land and with it an experience of justice or truth. At its root, to *recognize* is to come again to 'gnosis' – the word the New Testament uses for knowledge itself. Jesus brings with him the *gnosis* of God that saves us when it dawns on us – 'it's you!' – because it is the primal knowledge that is love.

'He came unto his own and the world did not know him …' In this failure of the world to recognize him, the tragedy of the story begins and inexorably descends into the utter dislocation and estrangement of Calvary. One could never do such a thing – the things done to victims and scapegoats from primordial times to Birchenau and Srebrenica – if one knew who they really were. Ignorance is the root of sin. And so, sin is healed by the illumination of knowledge, not just intellectual or factual but *gnosis* itself. Plato thought that all knowledge is a form of recognition. We were there once but, leaving that place of omniscience, we forgot most of it and landed in this condition of amnesia. But sometimes our memory is jogged and we are filled with knowledge again.

The Christian faith reflects this idea in a way. It begins with the birth of the all-knowing Word – the *Logos* that *is* knowledge – into the forgetful human condition. Although it doesn't say so explicitly it has to mean – and is assumed – that this newborn child was immersed in the amnesia of the human condition. Did the infant Jesus lie there crying but really thinking, 'So here I am, now let's get to work and save humanity'? No one recognized him. 'He came to his own and his own did not receive him.'

At the end of the story, in the Gospel of John, a successful recognition occurs. Several in fact, if one can really separate them, because they seem to be one collective experience as well as personal. This post-resurrection recognition bridges time and leads through the tragedy of the cross into the new world of saving knowledge. In this perspective, the universe story is a comedy. Tragic and farcical at times, it ends happily with a reunion. As in the greatest art, the tragic is not diminished but it is transfigured in a joyful climax that brings everything and everyone together. Separation and forgetting become the marriage of mutual recognition.

Grief-stricken, Mary of Magdala came to anoint the body of Jesus and found only an empty tomb. The angels she saw there were not much help to her. Then she *turned round* and saw Jesus 'standing there' (just *there* as if he had never been anywhere else). But 'she did not recognize him'. Tragedy and comedy begin to compete here. It's a sure sign that truth is coming. Jesus asks her the redemptive question found in many myths, a variation on 'How are you?' 'Why are you weeping? Who are you looking for?' Not what you would ask a perfect stranger unless you know that you are not a stranger.

Getting close to farce and building the tension, Mary, who is still thinking he is the gardener, grabs at a straw. Maybe this nice working man had for some reason removed the body. If so, could he tell her where he has put it? Jesus said, 'Mary.' He must have been looking at her and into her. She could only pay attention, and attention reaped her reward. Not for the first time, he turned a life around with a look. This time it was a recognition. She knew him then and said in Hebrew, '*Rabbuni*, Master.'

What happened? She knew herself known and the self-knowledge this sparked led her to a deeper knowledge of the *other* – of what we always think is unknowable and is indeed unknown to thought. This was an experience of re-connection with what had been lost and would also have been forgotten one day (eventually we forget everything that is not present). It sent a bolt of knowledge through her that pierced her ignorance and liberated her to recognize the one who had made it clear to her that she was known.

What an economical way to describe the resurrection. How else to describe it? There is no graphic account of the actual resurrection. No security camera in the tomb caught it. No 'wows', 'amazing', 'gee, what a surprise'. '*Rabbuni*', spoken in their shared language. He was there and she was there, nothing, no mistake or failure could separate them ever again. 'To the marriage of true minds there is no impediment.' Life went on as life must and yet it would never be the same again. 'He comes to us hidden,' Simone Weil said after he had visited her one evening in her room, 'and salvation consists in recognizing him.'

I was glad Burkard had said, 'Hello, Laurence', as I went to give my talk.

April 2009

29

The Imperial Throne

When you think about it, it is an extraordinarily daring assumption to declare a saint. It assumes you know how the next life, if there is one, is organized, with some degree of hierarchy. It is a kind of honour system that the English have perfected. But being a saint is more than a knighthood. It implies more than royal authority. And given the very human terrestrial organization that lies behind the canonization process it assumes great trust. In the end the question remains: does it really declare a choice of God's selective priorities or how a particular earthly institution sees things? Maybe the ambiguity of this goes to the heart of the nature of the pilgrim Church, ever a work in progress.

The 'causes' of saints – think of Pius XII and Oscar Romero, for example – are not exactly free of politics. Perhaps this is a reason why the canonization ceremony itself invests so much in the creation of atmosphere through the panoply of visible authority and solemnity. Balancing the hubris of claiming to know God's mind through an institutional medium and the humility of remaining a creature is the art of all theistic religion. Never more so than in this lottery of official sainthood.

During the ceremony, the Pope sits in the great solitude of his ancient primacy on an elevated *cathedra* in front of St Peter's. His supreme power is tempered by this sense of his personal loneliness. He looks down on the terraced ranks of the Church, clergy, religious and laity strictly segregated in the hierarchical order. This is the visible form of this Catholic part of the Body of Christ. Its image seared itself into the medieval mind and appears in countless paintings and literary work. It breathes the relief of an apparent, final status quo. Theology says all the parts are equal. But sacred theatre is not democratic. That is not possible as not everyone can sit on the throne. No one really wants it to be, actors or audience. Even Isaiah's vision of every hill laid low and every valley filled in seems a flatland of tedium. Drama requires at least the potential for conflict and competition.

Two superior acolytes are always beside the Pope. They hold up his vestments when he walks and hold the book he reads from. They imply that nothing can go wrong at this level. Two cardinals sit symmetrically below him, too close to the daily politics of the Church to be beside him in the sacred time of the liturgy. He is most distant from those he is closest to in the hierarchy. Everything in visible detail implicitly says something. There is a deeply satisfying sense of order that, in liturgical time anyway, overrides all the questions it raises. This is a unique kind of beauty that our secular age has forgotten. The time, effort and expense of this kind of ceremony affirms a level of cost-efficiency other than the financial.

The Roman aristocracy at a canonization carefully protect their ancient privileges, the ornate signs of which they wear proudly. Their presence is irrelevant to the main event but it asserts that the main event with its cosmic meaning is part of a context that includes local politics too. Ambassadors, military, politicians, all sit obediently in their right place. At this level, even a few women, with mantillas of course, come closest to the male pinnacle of power. The Swiss guards are almost invisible because they alone do not look at who is looking at them.

On the other side of the altar, the ecclesiastical hierarchy are ranked in descending order, cardinals, bishops, abbots, monsignori, each scrupulously identified by his vestments or robes. Less impassive than the guards, they *do* look around at those looking at them, smiling graciously at friends, looking blankly through strangers. In the square the people stand as the plebs must have done in ancient Rome, awed, excited, looking up, eager to be part of something so much more sublime than mundane life – a liturgy of public worship uniting heaven and earth. Between the highest and the lowest, more crowded and less comfortably seated are the monks, priests and members of the religious orders whose founders the Pope is inscribing among the saints of the Holy Roman Church.

Bernardo Tolomei, the founder of the Benedictine Monastery of Monte Oliveto Maggiore, the motherhouse of the Olivetan Congregation, was born in Siena, a city of saints, in 1272. His noble family was a pillar of the economic and political system and served as the Pope's bankers. He was a brilliant lawyer and joined a confraternity, one of the many devotional movements that swept Italy at his time. Suffering from damaged eyesight, a canonical impediment to ordination, he decided to withdraw from the world and settled with two companions in a remote part of his estates, the *crete senesi* on which the beautiful monastery still rests today. They lived in the spirit of the desert monks, and the simplicity and sincerity of their life led to the expansion of the community. Obedient to the local bishop's request, Bernardo gave a structure to their life and integrated it into the Church's institution by adopting the Rule of St Benedict. Later the Avignon Pope Clement VI recognized them formally. For some years, Bernardo, the acknowledged founder, declined to be abbot.

In 1348 the plague that was to devastate Europe, reducing the population by two-thirds, struck Siena. Bernardo, with some of his monks, returned to the city to tend and care for the sick. Catching the plague, he died with those he was caring for and his body disappeared into a common grave. The absence of relics impedes your *causa*.

Hagiography aside, it is difficult not to feel inspired by Bernardo Tolomei. He seemed genuinely averse to power even in the world he had created in his monastic family. Born to privilege he might have felt freed from the prison of hierarchy. Yet however intense this detachment, he lived it within the institution of the Church. Like Francis of Assisi and Catherine of Siena – and Italians today – he could see the dysfunctionality while loving the family.

In St Peter's Square that day we did the same. A curial cardinal once told me that only a sense of humour, renewed by frequent visits home, enabled him to survive Rome. In the sacristy before the ceremony the priests at the base of the hierarchy were being told the protocol for giving communion. 'You may even have a cardinal or bishop come to receive from you. Do not be frightened, give it to them in just the same way.' The priests laughed aloud reminding us that the Church in her wisdom recognizes that *hilaritas* is also a part of holiness.

May 2009

30

Anderson

Anderson was a golden boy. He was outstanding in his studies and the Marists who ran the school he attended in the Solomon Islands saw a great future for him. A future leader of his tropical paradise, maybe he would be one of the new generation to reverse the desperate corruption and exploitation of the poor that crippled the country's development like a cancer that refuses to be beaten.

He was bursting with youth and health and his sunny self-confidence made him a good winner. He always moved on quickly, eager for a new challenge rather than gloating over his successes. He was the kind of winner who did not care where his trophies ended up. His contemporaries liked to be in his entourage because success seemed to rub off from him. Or, perhaps it was just easier to live with your own mediocrity in the friendship of people with star quality whom you did not have to envy or worship from afar, but whom you genuinely liked and who, amazingly, seemed also to like you and count you as a friend. He was one of those rare souls who seem to be born as God's friend and never to have doubted it. He was handsome and athletic and loved to show off, especially to the girls. One of his performances was to jump off the back of a motor canoe as it crossed between the islands and then catch up with it with broad fast strokes and jump into the boat again, beaming with good-natured pride, shaking the water off himself like a magnificent god.

After another happy and brilliant term, Anderson said goodbye to his teachers and classmates. He made the long journey to his home in a poor and remote village on an island a few days' travel away. His parents and brothers and sisters and friends were eagerly awaiting him. Life was always richer when he was with them. He walked up the road to his house, greeting his neighbours with a smile and a wave. When he came to his own home he walked in through the front door, stumbled and dropped down dead.

There was no hospital or doctor to perform an autopsy, and burials happen quickly in the Solomons. The loss ripped into his family like a machete. There was more than grief, though; beneath the agony of their loss was a dark and frightening question. They contacted Fr Adrian at the school, who immediately made his way to their home and gave what comfort he could. Two weeks later the elders of the village convened to address the question that everyone was asking and no one had yet dared to raise. Not what, but *who* had killed the beautiful and gracious Anderson?

The elders of course knew everyone involved better than any outsider could, but their criteria for answering the riddle of Anderson's death drew not on medical science but on their ancient lore. They decided that the blame lay with the boy's father. Some months before, a Japanese film crew had come to their village asking about the dolphins about which they were making a documentary and which were numerous in the local waters, but only at certain times. Sharks were also the totem animal of the village. The Japanese had heard of the gift that some locals were reputed to have for 'calling' the sharks. They were referred to Anderson's father who used this gift for them – successfully, as it happened, for the film-makers and profitably for himself. The elders deliberating on the mystery of Anderson's death decided that the sharks were angry at being exploited in this way and, through the family's ancestors, they took their revenge through Anderson.

There could be no systemic forgiveness for the father after this verdict. Broken, guilty and desperate to escape the dark powers that had descended on him, he contacted Fr Adrian again and asked to be baptized. He went through the stages of preparation and embraced his new faith with relief. Shortly before the baptism he called Fr Adrian again and invited him to the village. He led him to a windowless hut where the skulls and relics of the ancestors were stored on shelves from floor to roof. Not daring to touch them himself, he pointed out the relevant ones belonging to his family to Fr Adrian who placed them in a bag and took them away.

When he returned to his church Fr Adrian buried the relics reverently in a plot of land near the cemetery. Later he picked up murmurings of disapproval and his successor was later asked to re-bury them more safely in consecrated ground. Anderson's father grew to become a committed member of the church and in time a catechist, breathing more freely in the faith that had rescued him from fear. Fr Adrian became archbishop, serving the gospel through the gift of his life to a people whom it takes a lifetime, or more, to understand. To Anderson's fading memory there still clings the enigma that all beauty and glory produce: what, on earth, is it *for*?

March 2009

31

The John Main Center

Silence is more than the absence of noise. As we sit twice a day in the John Main Center for Meditation and Inter-Religious Dialogue at Georgetown University, smack in the middle of a busy American campus, it is a drop of silence in an ocean of noise, a single breath of stillness in an endless gasp of activity. During the meditation session itself planes fly overhead at regular intervals and FedEx trucks crash gears as they reverse along the road outside. Students on their way to the library or dining room talk loudly in groups or on their cell phones. Usually the most important point occurs to them moments after they have separated and they turn back to shout their concluding remarks over the flight paths of other conversations and the silence of the meditation.

The John Main Center is the oldest building on campus, built in the same year as the White House. It has been a bakery, a stables, an infirmary and a computer storeroom. For the past few years students have enacted here what John Main believed, that 'there is nothing more important for men and women of our time than to rediscover the value and meaning of silence'.

It is a special grace for teachers of meditation to meditate with children or college students. The young today don't approach it with preconceived objections or anxious doubts. They accept it as a thirsty man takes a glass of water, as an opportunity to quench an overwhelming thirst. Although the Center teaches meditation from the Christian tradition, it is ecumenical in the widest sense. No expectations or demands of faith or belief are laid on those who come here to be silent in body and mind. The meaning of their experience of silence may grow after they have tasted it, as the real enjoyment of food comes after you have begun to eat it. Most of those who come regularly don't talk a lot about it, although they will say how important it is for them to have such a place to come to.

In meditation here they are not being evaluated or graded and they don't have to impress the teacher. It is not even something they can put on their résumé. Silence has a value but not on the same scale as other things in their lives. They don't talk much about their practice of meditation, but express gratitude for the daily support to persevere with it. Obviously many others on campus never do come to meditate – too shy, too busy, or just not interested – while others come to check it out and don't return. Many students and staff, however, now come to the Center alone outside the regular sessions when their own schedules allow. We decided to risk leaving the door open at all times and apart from the temporary theft of the meditation bowl it has been justified.

An actual center of contemplation on campus, dedicated to silence and complementing other kinds of campus ministry, has proved valuable and is well used. Other universities hear of it and are curious. Yet it is counter-cultural to most of the mores of student life and university institutionalism. It produces no immediately verifiable results and it cannot be measured by cost-effective means. This is true, in its own way, for every individual who meditates, as well as for the institutions – religious, corporate or academic – that make space for it.

The true silence of meditation is challenging in these ways. But it can also have a discomforting social impact. It exposes the false silences that distort and disrupt human relationships. Here in Washington DC, for example, there is a large African-American and Hispanic population. The great majority of them are in the service industries, doing the manual and menial chores the middle class don't have the time or taste for. Even in a university as sensitive to people and values as Georgetown is, these groups constitute most of the catering and maintenance staff but work behind a wall of silence separating those who serve from those who are served. There is also silence about the existence of this silence. When we become too busy for the true silence that reveals communion and nourishes community, we miss how we become trapped in the negative silence where communication is stifled.

As the desert monks knew, pride and greed are the greatest enemies of contemplation. Even in the competitiveness of the young student career these states of mind begin to overwhelm and blind us to alternative values. Mammon easily co-ordinates the forces of insanity, and locks us into our isolated envelopes of indifference. When we are blinded by desire and its close attendant, fear, our ability to pay attention to others is compromised. Most of the snatches of conversations you pass through on an American street are about money – prices of goods or personal debt, financial hopes or nightmares. On campus there is also, refreshingly, a lot about romantic desire (ideas are generally restricted to the classroom).

Yet if we do listen to the immigrants, politically noticed only when they ask for education and health services, we might learn something of real value. They have come here from real poverty and often live on the edge of poverty in order to support their families at home and the children they have here. It is a different set of concerns and values, another parallel universe. The more we learn what true silence means, the better we can hear what the poor are teaching us about true values and happiness.

Last week some Mexicans were painting in our house. When they finished their work I got into conversation with one and asked him to do a small extra job in the kitchen in his own time for which I would pay him. Before we discussed how much or when, he began to tell me about his life. He was in the country illegally, though working for a large company for less than the minimum wage. But he was hopeful in this land of optimism. He expected to get his papers soon so that he could visit Mexico and take his 5-year-old son to see his parents who had not yet seen their American grandson. I told him of my own Irish ancestors who had emigrated to the USA and found prejudice and resistance before they were able to establish themselves. In his poor English he had an openness and fluency that took us to a place of trust. He seemed to enjoy breaking through the wall of silence that normally separates him from his employers, and so did I. When he finished the job I had asked him to do I offered him his pay.

In a very un-American way he backed away and shook his head. I insisted and he refused again. 'No, it was a small job and we have spoken as friends,' he said. I was denied my small financial contribution to his struggle to survive but he arose far above it with a dignity on which no price could be put.

November 2007

32

Handicapped in Mumbai

Mumbai, cloudy, grey and damp, exuded the sense of disappointment and missed opportunity with which London frequently embraces its inhabitants. The difference was the clammy heat of the monsoon that pervaded every corner of every place and every inch of oneself. Rain fell in short intervals, sometimes in an intense deluge but mostly as heavy drizzle.

Sitting in an open motor rickshaw was cheaper and more fun than the air-conditioned taxis. The driver weaved in and out of traffic with a detached concentration showing neither impatience nor competiveness. Trapped inside, with the rain blowing in from both sides, at least we felt closer to the endless bustle of trade and travel on the streets. But by the time we arrived we were drenched. We had become part of the inescapable clinging dampness that was everywhere. As we walked into the air-conditioned building with our wet clothes clinging to our skin, the warm damp became cold damp and I felt like going back outdoors where you belonged to the humidity.

Talking about the season with the person who greeted us, I was told that Bombayites really like this kind of weather. It is cooler than the sweltering temperatures of summer and, above all, brings the water so desperately needed for the city reservoirs and the farmers out in the country. This year the disappointment was just that there was not enough of it, a soft, intermittent drizzle rather than the steady downpour they needed. I saw a different perspective, bigger than my own discomfort, and mentally stopped complaining.

We were visiting a home for the mentally and physically handicapped, founded by a determined woman who had made something remarkable happen against all the odds of prejudice and baksheesh. It seemed, at first sight, both well run and compassionate, making a small but effective response to this single aspect of the multiple problems of this city of 14 million – the world's second largest urban area after Shanghai. As we stood in the hall (more comfortable than sitting in wet clothes), listening to the history and the mission of the institute, a young student with disabilities came up and looked at us. Deciding that we were better than class, he sat beside us. We smiled at him and his face opened up in ecstatic happiness, until his teacher discovered him and gently teased and led him back to his studies.

We visited some of the classrooms. The teachers and volunteers teaching basic literacy to the disabled were prayerful, that is, simultaneously detached and committed. In the atmosphere of the learning groups there was an other-centredness that makes for good learning and good relationships. Their small groups of slow-learning students made small but real progress. The teachers were not well paid but were clearly rewarded by the incremental change they saw in their students responding to their devoted attention. The children wore school uniform because this hid the difference between those from middle-class families and the many others who came in daily from the slums and shanty towns. A shared handicap dissolves many barriers, including social status. It was not an overtly religious institution but it released a sense of the sacred, the unaccountable grace that moves among the wounded in the presence of compassion.

One of the volunteers was a young man with movie star looks and the confident charm that came with them. He came in several times a week to do something useful because he was unemployed. Although he didn't give them his full attention he was very popular with the children. He related to them more as an older brother than as a teacher. He did whatever he was asked to do by the staff, except to teach from books, because he himself could neither read nor write.

He was not the idle rich kid with an expensive haircut that he seemed. He had come to Mumbai from a tribal village in the far north of the country. His paler skin tone promised to get him on to the first rung of the ladder as he sought fame and fortune. Above everything he longed to be an actor. He dreamed of a few moments spent with a star that would change his life. He hung around the cafes where the Bollywood pantheon congregated. Occasionally he would get into one of the great parties that celebrated celebrity. Afterwards he returned to walk up dirty stairs to a single room on the top floor of a shabby house in a poor area of the city centre. He shared the room with fellow hopefuls, watching films, telling stories of lucky breaks. They lived on the phone. If they were not sitting on their mattress talking or sleeping or looking for work they were at the gym.

The secret handicap of this young man was also his greatest fear. It undermined even his fantasy of success. If he got a lucky break and found a part, how could he avoid eventually being exposed? He could not be stopped from walking into the best hotel and, for the time being anyway, his face was his fortune. But sometime someone would notice that he could not sign the register or read the menu.

Disadvantage comes in many disguises and the poor we will always have with us. Those who have not, even what they think they have will have it taken from them. As Mother Teresa often reminded the affluent, they may be poorer than those they help. For the degrees of poverty and the gap between the social extremes are frequently not what they appear.

Who can count how many people fall right off any social radar if they were never on it and no safety net was in place to break their fall? There are no forgiving nets here in space-age, high-tech India where the rich stroll along the Bandra promenade while a few metres away the poorest slum children play on the beach, where the contrasts are obscene. But so also is the conditioned ability of the haves to blank out the embarrassing, annoying reminders of what having nothing means, even the dignity of receiving common attention. The ancient poverty of the streets and slums seems the more outrageous for this inattention and, of course, because of the show-off extravagance of the wealthy.

What also shocks, however, is the lack of prophetic anger. Maybe it has been numbed or repressed. Or maybe, as we are often told, it's the belief in karma. But are we not allowed to be angry at karma? Perhaps the poor need the fantasy lifestyles of the rich and famous, the goddesses and gods of the screen, as an escape from the degrading realities of life. Simone Weil thought that day-dreaming is the root of all evil; but she acknowledged that it was the 'sole consolation of the afflicted'.

Maybe providing that false consolation just by their insensitive showing off makes some wealthy people feel better. Or perhaps it gives them a greater sense of security if the perceived gap between them and the poor is so extreme. By living so fantastically they feel they are making the daily shame of the poor a little easier to deny. The same argument is used to justify building great temples and marble-pillared churches among the dwellings of the poor, or erecting record-breaking Buddha statues in areas where whole villages get swept away in a year of heavy rains.

The unfairness of life is hard to live with. What makes it easier is not Bollywood or religious fantasy but the reality of one disabled person helping another, being open about one's shame at being unable to read or write, permitting the emergence of grace through a human wound.

August 2009

33

Stave *Church*

Providentially we were there over Midsummer Eve when the period of Scandinavian white nights would reach its zenith. And so, late and in a preternatural light, we walked up the hill to Hedalen church. It stands, squat and solid, commanding a beautiful view over the forested hills and valleys. Many generations of worshippers sleep in the surrounding graveyard. Hedalen is one of the 29 remaining wooden medieval churches of Norway, a survivor of more than a thousand constructed after Olaf Haraldsson returned home in 1015 with a new faith in the White Christ whom he was determined would drive out the old, dark Norse gods.

The Vikings had long ago perfected the arts of timber construction in shipbuilding. This was applied later to log houses, and then the *stave* churches adopted them to create these powerful, intensely *interior* places of Christian worship that were usually built on old Norse sacred sites. Externally they look like small, wooden versions of Thai temples, with their delicate elongated sweeps. But graceful as they are, with steeply ascending shingled roofs that look like pine cones, they are also heavily solid and grounded. Here in Norway they are the last of the wooden temples that were once to be found throughout Europe. They are called *stave* because of the *stafr* or load-bearing posts that in so virile a way embody the verticality of the theology.

The doorway into a Norwegian *stave* church is very narrow. Like everything else in this self-confident, self-contained architecture, the solid symbols of spiritual experience are making a point. It reminds anyone entering the church that entering the presence of God requires passing through a narrow portal of consciousness. We enter the sacred interior space of the Kingdom in solitude and with a minimum of baggage. The narrowness is single-pointedness. Then the worship conducted on the other side of the entrance will not be a superficial Sunday routine but a deep encounter bringing the personal psyche and the cosmos together into fuller resonance.

It is hard not to stop halfway into the body of the church, and not become absorbed in the elaborate carving round the portal, that *is* the portal, and try to decipher its narrative. After some study you can distinguish the dragons' heads and tails and trace them as they curl round each other in a frenzy of snarling, sneering battle. It is not just a conventional illustration of the duel of the forces of good and evil, as the ancient Norse would have seen it, but a more hopeful, Christian insight into the self-destructiveness of evil. These dark forces that separate us from the holy and the good spend themselves in violence at the entrance to the very place they came to destroy. But passing through and observing them is unsettlingly ambiguous. The battle is won but not yet over. What is going on inside of me as I walk into this inner room of prayer?

Inside the church you find yourself in the middle of a dense but peaceful forest, a human dwelling carved out in the heart of nature. Your eyes slowly accommodate in the darkness and you become a citizen of this new world that first arouses your sense of smell. Wood, tar, maybe the wool clothes of generations lost, and still a trace of incense. Originally in the late twelfth century it was a simple square room with a chancel for the altar, but the cruciform extension did not diminish its intimacy and immediacy. Near the soapstone font is a cheerful, rosy-cheeked Madonna and child commanding with a gentle authority. The crucifix over the altar is one of the great works of medieval art in Norway. The feet and toes of Jesus are spread out in graphic pain but the face has already found peace.

According to legend, the Black Death depopulated the valley in the fourteenth century. The forest encroached and the church was lost and forgotten. Two hundred years later a hunter shot an arrow at his prey and missed. As it flew into the dense forest he heard a metallic ring and discovered it had hit the church bell. Believing that the church belonged to a *huldra* or forest spirit he threw metal over the top of it and thus reclaimed it for human use. He walked inside and found a bear hibernating in front of the altar. He killed it and the skin still hangs in the sacristy (too small, though, to be my vestment for mass as I had hoped when I was told the story).

As several *stave* churches are associated with legends of animals being killed inside them it is possible to be sceptical about this one. Maybe some old Norse gods slipped through the portal of the writhing dragons and repeated a sacrifice in the style of the old dispensation. Gods, like people, as we know today, can feel nostalgic for old-time religion. Until recently, the legendary and pre-Christian survived in a tenuous friendship with the new faith. At midsummer the people of Valdres and Adal used to come to the church for several days of revelry (as Vikings, this meant drinking and fighting). The church atmosphere restrained but did not destroy this custom. But in the late nineteenth century a firmer pastor banned it and the old gods were finally expelled.

We were a different congregation that midsummer evening. New urban myths had replaced the old religious ones. Old certainties had confronted new doubts and new kinds of certainty had replaced them. But through all the passages of time, something - that the *stave* church embraces - is timeless. We broke bread and meditated after communion. Something the same yesterday, today and tomorrow, and present or waiting to emerge in every story by which we try to explain the mystery of the world and our place in it.

When we went outside again, the night was white.

July 2009

34

Maria's Mother

Determined not to let anything drop, like the born multitasker she was, Maria declined our offer to postpone the visit to her city. In addition to being a wife and mother and co-ordinator of the meditation groups, she was the principal carer for her slowly dying mother. Her children were also warmly engaged with the care and took on extra shifts to sit with their grandmother while their mother transported us from place to place for the talks and meetings.

Maria's mother had lain in bed at their home for months. She was not in pain or distress but slept deeply and, it seemed, drifted peacefully in and out of consciousness by day and night. Her spiritual existence seemed already to have migrated to a different level of consciousness, while her physical being remained, however tenuously, connected to that of this world – daily life filled with activity, juggling time, plans and problem-solving, keeping appointments and, very important in this Latin country, meal-times.

As we drove through the schedule of the visit, talks, meetings, a retreat day and sessions with schoolchildren, we received frequent reports on Maria's cell phone about her mother. They said 'no change, all is well, she is peaceful' – all especially reassuring to Maria as she invested herself fully on the plane of mundane existence. Yet, very obviously, she was never separated from her mother's presence and the peculiar blend of peace and fear that the process of dying can create.

On our last and very full day Maria asked us to her home for a late dinner with her family and some supportive clergy. We tried politely but unsuccessfully to decline. But it was clear she was set on it and we accepted. I should have remembered that the things we try to avoid often turn out to be the ones we never forget. So, though we were feeling more than ready for bed, we found ourselves sitting around a very well laden table with a large and very energetic, and energizing, group.

As the last course was being prepared and we were thinking to leave, Maria invited me to visit and pray with her mother. I was embarrassed to realize that I had sat through the meal half-forgetful of the dying woman in the same house. And I was further moved when I discovered that the room where she was dying was next to the one where we had all been dining so merrily. As we stepped into the sick room we were greeted by an atmosphere of expectancy and uncertainty that accompanies both the last phase of life and that of an approaching birth. It is a liminal experience: like being here and there at the same time, a frontier we are not sure has been crossed.

Maria's mother lay in a neat, well-made bed that showed the loving attention that had accompanied her these past months. Her head was resting peacefully on a pillow, seeming neither sick nor restless. She was breathing gently and calmly and her presence filled the room in an ego-less, undemanding way. Like the divine presence, it made no demands. Or, in its powerlessness, was it a total demand, both irresistible and unthreatening?

Maria and I sat beside her mother and meditated silently for some time. I then prayed in words and we returned to the silence. The old woman showed no response to our presence except perhaps through a deepening sense of her own presence. If it was communication it was in silence, the communication that *is* silence. After a few minutes we stood up to leave. I blessed the dying woman and Maria led the way out of the room. But, as I moved away from the bed, I looked back at her mother and saw that her eyes were wide open looking directly at me. It was a full gaze, very rare in this world, from an abyss filled with light. One might call it a blessing.

I called Maria back, but her mother's eyes had closed again. Intuitively we simply sat down again, not with any ritual intention, but just to be there. We needed to be there. It was our duty to be there and it was good to be there. In the full sense of the phrase, we were there to see what was happening. So, it was a moment, very rare in life, filled with the certainty that we were in the right place at the right time and we had nothing to do except to be fully present. The dying woman continued to breathe gently but the sensation of an imminent change became stronger. After a few minutes her breathing changed noticeably but not anxiously. Whatever we were meant to be there for was beginning to happen. There was a very strong sense of reality. She gasped for breath for the last time and then effortlessly yielded the instinct to breathe again. The instinct to survive surrendered itself into another kind of life against which it could not be measured. Her last breath opened a view of an existence without boundaries or forms, a dimension of perfect stillness, a holy finality that promised an everlasting beginning and that, at that instant, consumed all sadness and loss in a total silence.

The only moment of life that matches the drama of birth had come to pass. Just as at moments of deep prayer, emotion and thought became irrelevant. There was something more, less changeable and uncertain. Peace and joy rose from the abyss, a new presence out of the terrible absence. Maria's mother had finally died. Maria's loss was already being transformed.

February 2009

35

Shen Yeng

The city of Shen Yeng in north-east China has been settled for 7,000 years. So, there are many ancestors to venerate. The city was founded about 300 BC during the Warring States Period, at a time when the Britons had barely learned how to build hill forts. It had a noble history, becoming the imperial capital of the Qing dynasty before yielding to Beijing in the seventeenth century. Its prestige lasted long and faded slowly. Today it is an important industrial centre and indescribably drab – at least what I saw of it during a visit to its Catholic seminary.

The cold grey hand of communism can be felt everywhere, the effect of imposing a standard ideology on the diversity of human beings and their affairs. The architectural and urban uniformity is crudely plain, proud of its minimalist functionality. The style of another, more elegant and softer era occasionally shows through the cloak of sameness thrown over the city, visible in crumbling buildings or monuments that, like everywhere, local people walk past daily without looking at. The plain communist style expressed the ideal of equality of the Cultural Revolution. Like the perfect society of the western medieval Church, it proclaimed itself everywhere but was believed in fully by very few.

Yet the people of cities survive the worst that is done to them. The mood of the streets, the hawkers and busy pedestrians elbowing their way through the crowds, embody the culture that survives the worst of revolutions. What is it that allows a people to make it through the worst of its own mistakes and to rise from the humiliating ruins of its collapsed ideologies? After a break-down, what restores humour and civility, purpose, hope and the sheer drive to succeed? Immense energy, perhaps, as evident in the passionate, compulsive love of the Chinese to do business. This is manifested especially in family businesses, whether selling fruit or cell phone chargers on the street – or, indeed, producing cars in numbers that would destroy what is left of the US automobile industry if Chinese car manufacturers complied with US safety standards.

Surviving the tides of history also requires consistent, basic cultural habits, like food and the written, non-phonetic Chinese characters that are intelligible to the speakers of the many different Chinese languages. There are different styles of writing the characters but the meanings can be communicated everywhere. But food, in all its diversity and regional varieties, is the great cultural identifier. The Chinese say they will eat anything with legs, including the table. Halfway through one meal I was informed that I was chewing on Manchurian donkey, which made me look more closely at the shapes of the contents of the other dishes we were dipping into. Every meal is a new creation. It is the topic of conversation before, during and after it is eaten. Unlike the blandness of meat and two veg, burger and fries or curry and chips, ordinary people's food in China is a daily art, perhaps even a spirituality for a pragmatic people who do not spend time on religious metaphysics. The wisdom of food, like the wisdom of language, has passed with remarkably little change through space and time

The seminary was housed in a shabby business building in the city centre, seven floors of barely furnished rooms without elevators. So, even though the aesthetics were dispiriting compared with other standards, the students, staff and visiting lecturers get plenty of exercise. We felt sincere admiration for the resilience and determination of those who taught and studied in this place. In ways that the Western Church could benefit from seeing, the vocations in such Chinese seminaries are truly sacrificial. Religious freedom here is curtailed more than is publicly acknowledged. Yet, after decades of total repression, people have learned to play the system against itself. They tend to laugh rather than complain. Material comforts are minimal. Sharing in community what little they have is a way of life, reminiscent of the account of the early Christians in the Acts of the Apostles.

Although baptisms in the Catholic Church in China run far behind the Pentecostal churches, the Chinese Catholic Church here may one day dominate the universal Church, just as its economy has begun to do. Yet today it struggles to develop a balance in its religious and spiritual formation. It is very aware, to use the phrase most bishops and rectors used, of a 'lack of spirituality'. Experience of the contemplative dimension of the gospel and of prayer is waiting. But with typical Chinese determination they intend to fill this lacuna. In the Shanghai seminary I spent an intense day with very articulate fourth-year students and teachers discussing 'why meditation is prayer'. At the end of the day most of them said that they now believed it was and I learned much of what it meant in the process.

But the scale of the Church here is hard to imagine.

The new young bishop of Shen Yang travels around his vast under-resourced diocese like the provincial governors of the past. We went to visit him late in the evening in the cathedral house. We drove through almost empty, darkened streets and then turned off the main roads into shabby side roads that led, incongruously, to a large neo-Gothic church at the centre of the Catholic compound. As we waited for the gates to be opened by the night watchman, I noticed a shadowy figure moving around on the other side of the street. I assumed it was a homeless person preparing their bed for the night. Then I saw him light a fire in what seemed a ritualistic way and I was told he was venerating his ancestors.

At Chinese funerals toothbrushes, combs or (cardboard) computers are often placed on the coffin and (paper) credit cards or 'spirit money' are burned to make the deceased person more comfortable in their new world. The sense of a direct link between this world and theirs is vivid. Veneration of ancestors is most intense during the 49 days of judgement that follow death but it continues long after. The Chinese dead – like Christian souls – live on. Existing in layer after layer of generations, they can help us here and so we should remember them.

The fire crackled brightly in the dark street as the offerings were made and we waited to enter the cathedral. The continuities of history, stronger than the reigns of empires or even the ebb and flow of beliefs, were being threaded to the present.

November 2009

36

Mount Fuji

I had always wanted to see Mount Fuji. It is a sacred mountain, famous for its perfect cone shape and presence and it has been the subject of countless classical poems and paintings. Some of these I had read or seen but I had never visited the original. The mountain was one of those parts of consciousness that can seem more real than it really is.

I was invited to make it real by going to see it with a Buddhist priest who was responsible for a small temple in a town not too far from the mountain. With exquisite courtesy and gentle kindness he met us at the bus station. We were to visit his temple first and then join him and his family for lunch. *Temple* probably gives the wrong impression. It is a lovely Shintoist shrine of modest size, surrounded by urban dwellings and backyards. It would be better to think of it as a small parish church of no great ecclesiastical status.

This was the last day of my visit to Japan and I was quite perturbed by the oddness and complexity of Japanese culture. In Tokyo I had seen one, not very endearing, side. I had come to understand why a Catholic priest who had lived there for 50 years would not answer my question directly when I asked him if he now felt Japanese. He replied that the longer he lived there the more he understood what the Japanese really felt about foreigners. Except for one incident, when I had not removed my shoes in an establishment soon enough and thought I was going to be beaten for the transgression, I had encountered the formal courtesy of the people, but it felt just that, coldly formal.

My visit to Mount Fuji, the meeting with the Shinto priest and his family, were to make it all the more confusing. It was a revelation. Brief though the encounter was, I was touched by something in the Japanese spirit that explained why at least some westerners fall in love with the culture. Despite knowing that they will never be more than a marginalized foreigner they become entranced and attached to it for life.

While in Tokyo I had visited my friend William Johnston, the Belfast Jesuit who had spent a lifetime in Japan. He had barely survived the stroke that totally paralysed him some months before. He lay in the Jesuit infirmary, immobile except for his eyes searching for others, saddened, but still with his familiar twinkle. He would die – I prayed sooner rather than later – in the Japan he had admired and felt affection for but always knew he would never be embraced by. Bill Johnston had studied Zen in depth, though with reserve, and perhaps in this bare and minimalist practice he had found the secret of the culture.

Japanese religion is about coping with life in a dignified way but with a bare minimum of dogma and metaphysics. Ritual and aesthetics are more important than answers to the Big Questions of Life. 'Sincerity' means something different in a practice like this. Although the Shinto temple was a long way from classical Zen, the priest described his daily responsibilities with a clarity and focus that seemed revealing of more than what he was saying. Early morning and evening there were ritual prayers, the work of maintaining the building, listening to people's problems, visiting the sick. Familiar occupations of local religious institutions everywhere. He was calm and restrained, had humorous, observant eyes, and was flawlessly attentive and generous in his hospitality. He showed us the photo of his young wife who died recently. It sits on a shelf behind the main shrine area among the memorabilia of all the deceased members of his temple. His two sons are also priests now, having finished their studies, and his mother, who lives with them, comes from a priestly caste. It is a hereditary family business, as many European churches once were, a form of religion that makes the world it influences a more peaceful place.

They run the temple together in a way that seems wonderfully contented and peaceful, almost unconscious in their effortlessness. They had, perhaps unknown to themselves, created a little paradise. Our lunch was the most mindful meal I can remember eating. After lunch the father and his younger son, who poured the tea, celebrated the tea ceremony for us. It took place in a room dedicated for this purpose, which we had oddly to climb into through a small opening. Many Christians say they feel a resonance between this quintessential Japanese ritual and the Eucharist. It did make us immensely more present. The gentle, mindful naturalness of their celebration might well challenge the brusque way we often say mass. When the son made a slight error in the ritual – I could not see exactly what – his and his father's eyes met and I imagined he was about to be rebuked. But instead they smiled, even perhaps laughed a little and then continued with their natural seriousness.

The priest then drove us towards the cloud-topped mountain, warning us that as Mount Fuji was a feminine deity she was unpredictable and very often visitors come here but she does not allow them to see her summit. In fact, that day she was indulgent and we did see it, the bare, tapering slopes and the uneven, as yet unsnowcapped, peak of the volcano.

The memory of the priestly family and the oasis of their place of worship and work remained with me. It came strongly back to me when, soon after, I participated in Rome in the World Congress of Benedictine Oblates, many of them married followers of the Rule of St Benedict for Monasteries.

Speaking with monks around the world, I have seen how it is generally recognized that the old institutions are changing, some visibly crumbling, and yet also how often a denial of death prevails. Many of the less romantic or nostalgic oblates acknowledge this too. The older ones expect to pass on before the familiar forms of monastic life they have come to love will collapse. They are not so concerned about change. One told me how, when she visited the monastery, she loved to sit in the church before vespers identifying the approaching monks by the sound of their footsteps. For others, though, oblation is more about a contemporary spirituality, a way of life grounded in the wisdom of the ancient Rule, and a personal vocation.

We talk too much about the 'crisis of vocations' and often self-deceptively. The crisis is in our perception not the statistics, and reveals how slenderly we are often in touch with reality. New forms of monastic life are needed and inevitable. Ideally they are supported by the older institutions. In encouraging these new communities the declining monasteries practise the very renunciation of self-will they were established to allow. Benedict urges monks to welcome guests as if they were Christ himself. Well, sometimes it is the future that knocks on our door at inconvenient moments and asks to be admitted.

Even without the support of the old monasteries the new forms will come to birth because the archetype of the 'monk within' must seek expression and take form. Maybe the Shinto temple suggests one possibility for this. The world needs new forms of old religion that release peace as trees produce oxygen. In this way the small Shinto family temple I visited simply and very modestly tends to some of the needs of our ailing planet.

Contemplative life is marginal to the main forms and activities of religious institutions. But it is the central purifying element in religion. The new forms of religion may be smaller, more mixed and certainly more flexible in their ways of commitment and service. And so they will probably also be more focused in the contemplative experience that the world thirsts for today. Contemplation enhances every aspect of life – including, as Christians are coming to see, family life. It sharpens the perception of time but reduces the speed at which we pass through it. In these new forms of religion maybe we will again find the space necessary to share tea and to say mass with delight.

October 2009

37

Fara Sabina

Mindful motion. Walking in a slow rhythm, in a large circle with others, on a balcony with a panoramic view over the rolling, easeful beauty of the Roman *campagna*. A distraction became a train of thought, diminishing my mindfulness.

In the late 1970s, when I left England with John Main to open a new monastic community, I wrote to a young fellow monk to tell him of all that was happening in my life and that of the new community. It must have caught him at a bad moment as he replied very tartly, thanking me for the news but adding that, in his opinion, in 'the real monastic life nothing ever happens'. This – and life's diverging directions – took the wind out of the sails of our friendship.

He went on to high administrative office on the monastic stage, so I wonder if later he changed his mind about the life where nothing happens. His remark remained with me, not only because it was rather hurtful at the time but also because in a way I agreed with him. Of course in life something is always happening and the attempt to pretend otherwise is false contemplation. But the idea that nothing happens remains strangely attractive. Maybe it is an insight into balance and harmony undisturbed, though not insulated against external stimulus. About perception of reality rather than merely 'events'.

I remember visiting a monastery long before I even thought of becoming a monk. While waiting for someone, I was watching the monk who was the porter sitting at his desk by the front door ready for anything but, at least in the time I was there, never called upon to respond to bell or visitor. No doubt he was a good porter, but he certainly wasn't multitasking. The person I was with also noticed the slow progress of this uneventful job and made an easy joke about the inactivity of the monastic life. It is an obvious way of making fun of this odd way of life whose purpose is not easy to see – even, at times, when you are living it.

I joined in the joke at the time but also realized to my surprise that I did not truly agree with it. I thought I saw a purpose and value in doing if not exactly nothing then at least not very much. Doing one thing at a time looks like doing nothing. It held an unexpected attraction for me even then and later I found it at the heart of what John Main, my teacher in this form of life, taught me. It was an early, inexperienced glimpse into the meaning of contemplation as taught by Jesus who said to Martha, the typical burned-out multitasker, that 'only one thing is necessary'.

This old memory slid into my mind on the balcony where we were doing our contemplative walk. I was coming to the end of a week-long meditation retreat with a group of 40 teachers (from 15 countries) of the tradition we practise in the World Community for Christian Meditation. We call it a 'School Retreat' after St Benedict's term for the monastery as a 'school of the Lord's service'. There were four clergy and the rest were a cross-section of the Body of Christ, representing many relationships to the institution and many forms of life. Nothing happens during the retreat. We meditate and walk, listen to a short talk, celebrate an almost silent mass. And eat and brush teeth and perform other necessities of nature. But the point is less about doing these things as about shedding as much unnecessary activity – mental and physical – as possible. Such a way of spending a week might appear either sublime, self-centred or plain pointless depending on your perspective, your length of experience in meditation or, as with my friend of many years ago, your mood of the moment.

Apart from a short personal interview each day, a short conference and the very quiet mass with meditation after communion, we observed complete silence. In shorter weekend silent retreats people struggle to practise silence and are just about getting into it when the retreat ends. But in the School Retreat it is strange to see how deeply people slip into the silence and find it a way of communion rather than isolation. The conferences I gave were about the nature of faith and belief and the distinction between them. So, a little mental exercise connecting with the challenges of Christian identity today, but not too heady or argumentative. The point of the retreat is not the labour of thinking but the *work* of contemplation. Origen, an early Christian monk, described prayer as the 'laying aside of thoughts'. This is not, as it may sound to some, a way to gibbering mindlessness but, quite the reverse, to a very powerful state of awareness and alertness. We meditated seven times a day, interspersed with the mindful walk on the balcony with the vast view. Minimum reading was recommended.

It was wonderful to see how everyone slipped so readily into this engaged non-action, which is as different from *inactivity* as it is from *hyperactivity*. We all found this meaningful but, of course, not everyone found jumping in at the deep end of the pool of prayer to be easy. One woman told me that though she was glad she had done the retreat and understood meditation better she wouldn't do it this way again, thank you. But, as was evident in the short daily interviews, most people following this interior pilgrimage opened like flowers in sunshine. They expanded emotionally and spiritually, finding a new level of peace and joy and renewed meaning for their life, work and family. Desires and anxiety diminished as the panorama of the Spirit expanded. Things fell into perspective. One person coming to the retreat with a lot of anxiety during a difficult transition in his career fell unexpectedly into the peace that lies beyond understanding. He found that this peace also underlies all good and balanced judgement.

The discovery that happiness does not consist in the multiplication, or even in the satisfaction, of desires plunges those who experience it into the mind behind the Beatitudes. Deep shifts of consciousness can happen in the silence of a retreat where nothing happens. Maybe for some it is temporary and for others an irreversible milestone. For us all, though, life became simpler and faith deeper. Reflecting on the relationship between faith and belief, Karl Rahner's insight seemed even truer, that the Christian of the future will be mystical – or nothing.

On the last night we celebrated the Vigil Mass for Pentecost with a special kind of liturgical love. As we prayed the Our Father in our different tongues, from Aramaic to Swahili, we could hear the harmony of differences, the prayer of tongues and the music of the Spirit that is so easily drowned in the busy blare of our media-saturated minds. A life in which 'nothing happens'.

June 2009

38

Montserrat

On my way back to my hotel that evening I was swallowed up in a great football liturgy. Thousands of Barcelona FS fans poured on to the streets of their home city to celebrate a victory. In classical Rome, liturgy (*leitourgia*) originally meant the public celebration of a duty. But on the streets that night, as I gave up fighting my own way through the crowd and surrendered to its collective mind, duty did not seem the best word to describe what people were feeling. It was not an obligation imposed by inner or outer compulsion but an intoxicating and irrepressible inner impulse driving a tidal movement in which each individual was but a single wave.

The joy of the crowd, which each person was bound to express with the full power of their freedom, had moved beyond competition. For now, it did not need to look for opponents to fight and prove itself against. The crowd's exuberance was benevolent, good-natured. There were no enemies, and strangers could be tolerated because they were ignored. It did not need alcohol to fuel its euphoria. The roar of praise and adulation that greeted the appearance of the godlike members of the winning team on a huge screen in the open square, the dancing in the fountains, the flag-waving fans climbing the statues: it was a liturgy from the heart, convincing people they were one as no other religion could any longer do.

Barcelona is the capital of Catalonia, a fiercely independent part of Spain that is proud of its history and often scornfully indifferent to the institutional church. During the Franco dictatorship the Church legitimized the regime in return for financial subsidies, comfortable status as the official religion and conformity of civil law with Catholic dogma. It might have seemed a dream for the institutional church and an arrangement any national church, even in many countries today, might envy still. But it was a nightmare of the spirit and a double-edged sword severing the people from a feeling of connection to their church. Some of the movements that arose in the Spanish church during these years became globally influential – Josemaria Escrivá, the founder of Opus Dei, enthusiastically praised Franco's regime – but the hearts and minds of most Catalans and their children were lost.

The notable exception to this indifference to the old religion is the ancient Benedictine Abbey of Montserrat, an hour's drive from Barcelona, built high and deep into the rock face of the jagged mountain range. The word Montserrat means serrated mountain, like a saw and that is how the many peaks of the mountain seem, silhouetted against the skyline.

The morning after the ecstatic soccer liturgy I went to this quieter place of myth and political courage. Some Arthurian legends locate the Grail here, and the Black Madonna, before whom Ignatius of Loyola prayed on his way to Manresa, still attracts busloads of devotees. During the Franco years it resolutely defied the repressive regime and maintained the Catalan language and culture against those who tried to eradicate it. The government dared not attack the monastery directly but its security forces would lie in wait at the foot of the mountain and arrest the poets and political leaders when they came down from their meetings in the monastery.

The monastic community today is still robust, self-confident and – rare enough for monasteries today – seems to know who it is and why it is there. Each day after the midday prayer the Escolonia, the famous boys' choir, sing the Salve in Catalan under the statue of the Madonna. It is a powerful little liturgy in a moving place of worship that brings culture, faith and religion together in an experience that feels completely contemporary – tradition without nostalgia. As I stood on the balcony at the back of the basilica and watched the crowds below pray and the choir form in front of the statue and sing from its heartfelt national pride, I felt intrigued that the street liturgy of the previous night was not estranged from the liturgy in the church. They were different kinds of celebration but the roots of this religion could still draw from the life, the culture, of the people.

I was trying to understand this when I realized the third dimension that made this marriage of religion and culture so energized. A thousand feet above the monastery, reached by a steep flight of steps cut into the rock of the mountain, some cave hermitages look down over the monastery and onwards towards the city of Barcelona. When the Dalai Lama visited the monks here he asked to speak with Dom Basili Girbau, a well-known and respected hermit of great influence throughout Catalonia. He told me he had asked the learned and solitary Benedictine monk what he did all day and the reply was 'I meditate'. 'What do you meditate on?' the Buddhist monk asked him. 'Love' was the reply. The Dalai Lama said he looked into the hermit's eyes and knew immediately and for certain that he was telling the truth.

City crowds, monastic communities and then, in high and remote dwellings, hermits. What do hermits do? Like *sannyasi*, wandering renunciants in Indian tradition, Christian hermits are free spirits. St Benedict saw the communal life as a preparation for the 'single-handed combat of the desert'. In solitude the monk has no one to blame for his own faults; psychological projection is not possible and he has to face himself as he really is. They evolve in community and then, but without being uprooted from relationship, they soar in a cosmic liberty of spirit. It is a powerful, mysterious form of spiritual life and a strange but effective form of witness to ultimate values because it reconciles the polarities of community and solitude. By disconnecting, the hermit connects.

Hermits have lived on the mountain of Montserrat since the sixth century, even before community life was established there, long before the Madonna and the coach parties. Solitude engenders community because hermits draw people to them precisely because they do not seek to. Over time a relationship is formed between the solitary and the community. This itself is a witness and during Spain's hard years of dictatorship it connected with a desperate generation.

Dom Basil and the other hermits of Montserrat had transcended religious forms without rejecting them. Their simple religion had a pure authority, like that of the religion of Christ. It did not seek special accommodation with the powers of the world but defended truth against the mendacity of injustice and oppression.

Early Christians believed in three kinds of liturgy: the liturgy of heaven, the cosmic praise of the creation to the creator; the liturgy of the altar, celebrated in daily life by ordinary people; and the liturgy of the heart that unites heaven and earth. The hermitages at the top of the mountain make a hard climb but the view at the top is abundant reward.

June 2010

39

Aisling

Aisling (pronounced Ashlin) is an Irish name meaning beautiful dream or vision. That she was, for her parents Jack and Anne Sullivan, her four brothers and all who knew her. She was a blonde-haired sprite, perfect, filled with an infectious love of life and adventure and innocently confident of her charm. She loved everything pink. She loved to dance, to make candy floss, to meditate, to have her favourite stories reread to her, to tumble with her loving brothers.

A few days before her fatal accident, aged five and a half, she got out of her mother's car by the pier on Bere Island. To Anne's terror she leapt up on the wall overlooking the water and began to walk on it, poised over the long drop with the blissful exuberance and self-confidence of a child unaware of danger and mortality. She was talked down and later, to teach her the lesson, she was grounded for five minutes in her room.

A loose piece of masonry, an accident unpredictable and unblameable, ended her days in this world. Dancing around in their sitting room she pulled down a mantelpiece on her golden head. She lay so quiet and seemed so physically unhurt by it that her father thought she was playing still. When he saw some blood in her ear he realized what had happened and ran down the road with her in his arms to his boat. Word quickly reached Anne who joined him on the boat and took Aisling in her arms. As soon as she saw her, she realized as a nurse and as a mother, but without losing hope in the impossible, that it was too late; Aisling's spirit, or at least her brain, was gone. For a few days the residual activity of a small amount of electricity in the brain stem kept her on life-support. The technology surrounding her frail, peaceful body seemed out of proportion to her small size compared with the machines and tubes helping older patients in the ICU. Nature and science were in opposition. Scans showed her brain was irreparably damaged. Breathing support and IV kept her breathing.

But the technology was part of a broader picture of meaning. The machines gave time, precious time, to absorb the sheer impact of trauma, for the extended family and friends to gather in support and for her parents and brothers to begin the years needed to adjust to the abyss that had so suddenly appeared among them and in an instant changed their lives for ever. There are few moments in life when you know instantly and for certain that you will never be able to forget what is happening or, however terrible the happening, that you will even want to forget. In these moments you are reduced, humbled before the immensity of the ocean of the cosmos through which our little ship is passing. We may be citizens of this world but we have no rights against its laws. In such times we glimpse the vast fragility, tenderness and terrible beauty of being human.

Nature and technology complied and Aisling died in the arms of her parents. Her brothers, wisely counselled how to approach the unfathomable loss, helped to wash her body. This was Ireland, where death and the dead body are not airbrushed out of life. When they returned home to the island they found that neighbours and friends had cleaned the house, stocked the cupboards, prepared several meals for the days ahead, cut the grass and made up extra beds for the American relatives. The priests were talking behind the scenes, preparing for the liturgy, integrating the wishes of the family but also addressing the collective grief that had struck everyone in the small island community.

The wake lasted several days because so many came to pay their respects, to sit in silence in the room where the accident had happened and Aisling was laid. Old people who were Anne's patients from town and who hardly left their own house except to go the doctor made the ferry trip to the grief-stricken home. A neighbour in a feud with Jack walked down the road and, in the sadness that was greater than any anger, was reconciled. Dormant friendships revived. A look, a hug, a few words thrown like a thin bridge across the gulf of silence. When a heart is broken it sends tremors through all surrounding hearts.

'How else but through a broken heart may Lord Christ enter in?' wrote Oscar Wilde in the ruins of his life. Heartbreak somehow makes a way to open deeper centres of consciousness. It seeks healing and meaning in the chaos. Hearts are 'touched' not addressed. They cannot escape the truth that has touched them. But compassion from others, the pure attention we give to a fellow human being in great distress, gives hope that the pain and despair of a broken life may transform. We feel a strange response to those who have been in the firing line of tragedy and barely survived. The usual line of otherness separating us from people becomes very thin and we see others in ourselves and ourselves in others. Tragedy opens us to a sense of mystery and reverence. Aisling had unknowingly blessed others with her brief but joyful life. One could believe that she would continue to do so even through the awful absence of her death.

Human empathy is a force of nature. When it is awakened an unpredictable – and what may seem at first a foreign – energy enters the devastated system that was once a normal life. We call it grace. Tragedy hurls us to the terrifying cliff edge that in fact we always tremble on in every moment. As we fall over it a new world takes shape.

These ineffable, almost unwanted but tangible touches of grace in the midst of a tragedy demand and seek expression. The funeral mass and the local traditions enacted in the small island church spoke a formal language to express the intimate loss. It was a blend of ancient ritual and the personally spontaneous. People spilled out of the church not as, so often, from a sense of duty but needing to express their solidarity. Those standing outside heard the service through the speakers provided by Josie, the island's DJ.

June 2010

40

Skellig

Our small boat ploughed its disappearing furrow through rough waves to the pyramid of Skellig Rock. An English pilgrim, in an irritated voice, uncertain what pilgrimage meant and how it differed from tourism, asked, 'What on earth made them come out here?' She meant the Celtic monks who, between the sixth and thirteenth centuries, prayed on top of this 700-foot sea-battered rock island that soars up out of the sea 13 miles off the coast of Kerry. If there was an answer to her question it was lost in the wind and spray. An Irish cousin looked at her and nodded knowingly but said nothing. He had replaced the white magic of Irish Catholicism with New Age charms. Skellig, he thought, was on a lay line of cosmic energy. But there was a better understanding in him about the extraordinary place we were visiting.

The best answered prayers are those that have never been asked. So we felt pure gratitude as the sun suddenly appeared and burned away the grey clouds that had been hiding it since morning. We completed the trip to the Rock in the glory of the day, a vast blue sky decorated by big white cumulus, a calm but heaving sea coming closer to the two Skelligs, the smaller a bird sanctuary, the other a sanctuary of the soul's encounter with God.

When we jumped from the boat on to the rock we were met with official warnings. Two tourists had died on Skellig last year. People with heart conditions or afraid of heights were advised to look and enjoy but not climb further. The custodians of the island were archaeology students who seemed to feel it a special privilege to be there. The lighthouse on the other side of the island is now automatic but in the past three keepers and their families lived here for weeks at a stretch. They received their provisions from the visits of the ships of the Irish Lights, the captain of one of which had been my grandfather Mike Sullivan. Three keepers were necessary in case one went off his head and the other two could overpower him. Perhaps for the same reason, they still have three custodians. The archaeologists may also be secretly driven by the same hunger for solitude as the lighthouse keepers and their monastic predecessors.

Almost anything we say about the history of Skellig is uncertain. Like the historic sites of the Holy Land or the 'what really happened here?' element of the gospel stories, it doesn't matter as much as it seems at first. What matters is how present you are to what the place – or the story – is saying to you now. The climb up the 500 rough-hewn steps is hard work, a tiring allegory of the ascent of the soul to the peak of God. As on that journey, there are occasional resting places but no turning back. As the old rabbi said, God does not expect us to succeed but we are not allowed to give up.

What kind of success did the monks who came here want? What wrestling with their egos took place as they tried not to give in to despair, impatience or pride? To survive, they must have become very familiar with their egos and those of their companions. I could see my own possessive ego aroused when other visitors got in the way of my view or my thoughts or interrupted the rhythm of my ascent by blocking the steps to take photos.

The monks had lived in a compact walled enclosure of six drystone, efficiently waterproof beehive huts. One of them was the kitchen and common space, and there were two oratories in a sheltered corner of the peak. One of many legends (dating back to 1400 BC) says that Daire Domhain, a 'king of the world', came here to recoup his strength before an epic battle. If his title seems inflated it may be only that he felt he really was on top of the world as he looked around him from Skellig's summit over the ocean and to the end of the sky.

What is most striking here is the paradox that this remote and often completely inaccessible place was a home both of solitude and of community. If you wanted to get away from it all, why come to the top of a rock in the middle of the Atlantic with a group of 12, sharing a hut with two other solitaries? There are remains of a single hermitage at the top of the south peak but the main enclosure was for praying and living alone together. There was a common life punctuated by meals and prayers and there were certainly chores. What life is without chores? There are signs of burials in the tiny cemetery, of planting in a small vegetable garden with thin soil, of collecting gulls' eggs and rainwater in a stone cistern. This is not the solitude of the 'single occupancies', the bedsit or bachelor apartment of urban individualism. How ordinary this extraordinary life must have been here.

So, yes indeed, 'What on earth made them come out here?'

If you put your camera away and if you spend half an hour inside one of the huts you may feel an answer forming in yourself. It may be repulsion or exhilaration. Either they were crazy sociophobes or, on the mainland, they had already found something that they came here in order to be with more completely. Their community was an essential part of their solitude because in the solitude of their deepest selves they had found relationship. It was endurable here because they had already fallen in love with the one love that you can never fall out of love with. They would have seen this daily in their brethren.

When the monks left Skellig in the thirteenth century it became a place of pilgrimage associated with hard penance. Since then it has become a World Heritage Site and a place for off-the-track tourists. But before all that, it was a sanctuary of love, the more intimate because of its remoteness.

August 2010

About
The World Community
for Christian Meditation

John Main founded the first Christian Meditation Centre in London in 1975. The World Community for Christian Meditation (WCCM) took form in 1991 after the seed planted then had begun to grow into a far-flung contemplative family. It now continues John Main's vision of restoring the contemplation dimension to the common life of the Church and to engage in dialogue in the common ground shared with the secular world and other religions.

The present director of the Community is Laurence Freeman, a student of John Main and a Benedictine monk of the Olivetan Congregation. The International Centre of the World Community is based in London, with centres in many other parts of the world. The Community is a 'monastery without walls', with both developed national organizations and emerging communities in over a hundred countries. A major building block of all this is the growing number of small, weekly meditation groups which meet in homes, parishes, offices, hospitals, prisons, and colleges. They form an ecumenical Christian community of diverse gifts and traditions.

Annually the John Main Seminar and The Way of Peace events bring meditators together in dialogue with other traditions and global movements. The Community also sponsors retreats, schools for the training of teachers of meditation, seminars, lectures, and other programmes. It contributes to interfaith dialogue particularly, in recent years, with Buddhists and Muslims. A quarterly spiritual letter with news of the Community is mailed and also available online. Weekly readings are available by email, and a growing number of online resources are being developed to help the spiritual journey with the use of latest technology. This enables new initiatives such as teaching of meditation to children, networking young adult spirituality, and the contemplative dimension of the life of priests. Medio Media is the publishing arm of the community, producing a wide range of books and audio-visual titles to support the practice of meditation.

Meditatio is the outreach of the World Community, initiated to mark its twentieth anniversary. Co-ordinated from the Meditatio Centre in London, a programme of seminars brings a spiritual approach to key social issues of our time such as education, mental health, peace and justice, business, care for those in recovery and the dying. Meditatio is developing the use of technology in the work of spiritual renewal. It will also help with the formation of a younger generation of meditators who will serve later as leaders of the community.

The World Community for Christian Meditation: www.wccm.org.

The World Community for Christian Meditation Centres and Contacts Worldwide

For more information about the Community, its work and publications, to join a meditation group, or to learn to meditate, please contact your country co-ordinator or the International Centre.

International Centre
The World Community for Christian Meditation
32 Hamilton Road
London W5 2EH
United Kingdom
Tel +44 20 8579 4466
welcome@wccm.org
www.wccm.org

National websites linked to the World Community for Christian Meditation

(for countries not listed below contact the International Centre)

Argentina	www.meditacioncristianagrupos.blogspot.com
Australia	www.christianmeditationaustralia.org
Belgium	www.christmed.be
Brazil	www.wccm.com.br
Canada English	www.wccm-canada.ca
Canada French	www.meditationchretienne.ca
Chile	www.meditacioncristiana.cl
China	www.wccm.hk
Colombia	meditacioncristianacol.blogspot.com
Denmark	www.kristenmeditation.org
France	www.meditationchretienne.org
Germany	www.wccm.de
Hong Kong	www.wccm.hk
Indonesia	www.meditasikristiani.com
Ireland	www.christianmeditation.ie
Italy	www.meditazionecristiana.org
Latvia	www.jesus.lv
Malaysia	www.wccmmalaysia.org
Mexico	www.meditacioncristiana.net
Netherlands	www.wccm.nl
New Zealand	www.christianmeditationnz.org.nz
Norway	www.wccm.no
Poland	www.wccm.pl
Portugal	www.meditacaocrista.com
Singapore	www.wccmsingapore.org
South Africa	www.wccm.org.za
Spain	www.wccm.es
Spain Catalonia	www.meditaciocristiana.cat
Ukraine	www.wccm.org.ua
United Kingdom	www.christianmeditation.org.uk
United States	www.wccm-usa.org
Venezuela	www.meditadores.blogspot.com